Guide to Basic Edition

SO-DYU-746

BURNS/PELTASON/CRONIN

GOVERNMENT BY THE PEOPLE

Bicentennial Edition 1987-1989

Thirteenth Edition

Raymond L. Lee

Indiana University of Pennsylvania

Dorothy A. Palmer

Indiana University of Pennsylvania

Prentice-Hall, Inc., Englewood Cliffs, New Jersey 07632

© 1987, 1985, 1984, 1978, 1975, 1972 by Prentice-Hall, Inc.
A Division of Simon & Schuster
Englewood Cliffs, New Jersey 07632
Previous editions, titled Guide to American Government,
  1969, 1966, 1963 by Prentice-Hall, Inc.

Printed in the United States of America

10 9 8 7 6 5 4 3 2 1

ISBN 0-13-361627-4 01

Prentice-Hall International, Inc., London
Prentice-Hall of Australia Pty. Limited, Sydney
Prentice-Hall Canada Inc., Toronto
Prentice-Hall Hispanoamericana, S.A., Mexico
Prentice-Hall of India Private Limited, New Delhi
Prentice-Hall of Japan, Inc., Tokyo
Prentice-Hall of Southeast Asia Pte. Ltd., Singapore
Editora Prentice-Hall do Brasil, Ltda., Rio de Janeiro

Contents

Preface

The basic goal of this new edition of GUIDE TO GOVERNMENT BY THE PEOPLE is that of its predecessors -- to offer the reader a rational way to learn about American Government. To that end we have tried to focus on the most significant aspects of each chapter of the text. In the final analysis we believe that all true education is self-education. Students can claim no concept as their own until they can use it. We hope to shorten that process by making students their own tutors.

We owe a long-term debt to those students and teachers who have taken time to write us about the strengths and weaknesses of this Guide since it was first published in 1963. But obviously our greatest indebtedness is to Professor James MacGregor Burns of Williams College, President J. W. Peltason, American Council on Education, and Professor Thomas E. Cronin, Colorado College. Their lively, insightful approach to American government is the basis of this workbook. GOVERNMENT BY THE PEOPLE is in its fourth decade and thirteenth edition, still displaying all of its original zest.

We also owe a debt to our colleagues, whose ideas we have shamelessly pirated. Especially worthy of mention is Professor Bert A. Smith of IUP, a skillful, seasoned teacher who has used various versions of the Guide for over a quarter century. Finally, no list of acknowledgements would be complete without citing our secretary, Kathy Nowinsky, who has converted our crabbed, barely legible handwriting into manuscript pages from which publishing was possible.

Indiana Pennsylvania

Raymond L. Lee
Dorothy A. Palmer

How to Use This Guide

This Guide is designed to supplement and complement James MacGregor Burns, J. W. Peltason, and Thomas E. Cronin's GOVERNMENT BY THE PEOPLE, 13th edition. It should speed your out-of-class preparation and improve your test performance when used in a variety of ways: while you are studying; as you finish a chapter; or to review several chapters in preparation for an exam. We would like to suggest a basic study plan that most students have found to be very successful.

First, examine the Chapter Outline in the Guide to get an overview of the text chapter you are about to read. Next, take the Pretest. After checking your answers (found at the end of each chapter), read the text chapter with the outline in mind, concentrating especially on those sections where you may have missed Pretest questions. Now, retake the Pretest and check all missed answers. Move on to the Programmed Review section, again rechecking all missed answers in the text. Lastly, take the Posttest, using the same procedure.

Finally, examine all items in the Key Concepts section until you are confident that you have a suitable answer for each item in mind.

Before each major unit test, recheck your knowledge by reviewing all questions in the pertinent Guide chapters.

May we wish you "Best of Preparation" for this course, rather than "Best of Luck."

1 The Making of a Republic—1787

Americans are governed under a written constitution that is two centuries old. The original document has been amended and interpreted since 1787 to make it conform more nearly to American goals of openness, representation, and responsibility. That search in one sense is the very essence of American democracy. In this chapter, we look at how the framers approached the problem of building a strong national government and at the background from which the federal Constitution came. Above all, our constitution is a living, changing document, rather than a faded parchment scroll.

CHAPTER OUTLINE

   I. A CONSTITUTIONAL BICENTENNIAL

  II. A CONSTITUTIONAL GOVERNMENT
     A. Two central principles: division of powers; separation of powers
     B. Basic democratic premises: importance of individual, equal rights, individual freedom
     C. Liberty and equality
     D. Basic democratic processes: equal voting rights, access to competing ideas, right to organize politically, majority rule

 III. ORIGINS OF THE AMERICAN REPUBLIC
     A. A conservative revolution
     B. Weak central government under the Articles (1781-88)

C. Constitution drafted, Philadelphia Convention (1787)
D. Intention: to create stronger constitutional republic
E. Compromises: representation, taxation
F. Disputed motives of framers: idealism v. self-interest
G. The collective genius of the framers

IV. THE ADOPTION DEBATE
A. For adoption: Federalists (city and seaboard); opposed: Antifederalists (back-country farmers)
B. The Federalist
C. Antifederalist demand for a bill of rights
D. Ratification within a year (1788)

V. INTO THE THIRD CENTURY
A. The evolving Constitution
B. Open representation and accountability still unresolved
C. Maintaining a republic

PRETEST

1. One of the following words is not at the heart of American beliefs.

   a. competition   c. liberty
   b. freedom   d. equality

2. When democracy is described as a process, we emphasize

   a. equal voting rights.   c. individual freedom.
   b. worth of the individual. d. liberty and justice.

3. Advocates of democracy argue that the public interest is best discovered by

   a. consulting top social   c. entrusting decision making to
      scientists.   political party leaders.
   b. permitting all adults to d. the creation of philosopher-
      have a vote.   kings.

4. Democracy as a theory of government is centered on

   a. the individual.   c. interest groups.
   b. political parties.   d. an independent judiciary.

5. Constitutionalism as a part of democratic government serves to

   a. define and limit the   c. protect the rights of the
      government's power.   majority.
   b. expand the authority of d. safeguard against revolution.
      officials.

6. Under the Articles of Confederation, government power was concentrated in

    a. the president.   c. the people.
    b. the courts.   d. the state legislatures.

7. The historian who argued that the founding fathers wrote the Constitution to protect their property rights was

    a. Diamond.   c. McDonald.
    b. Brown.   d. Beard.

8. The American Revolution is best described as

    a. conservative.   c. radical.
    b. bloody.   d. reactionary.

9. The best characterization of the framers of the Constitution would be

    a. visionary idealists.   c. experienced, practical
    b. political philosophers.   politicians.
                                     d. spokesmen for the average
                                        person.

10. The Three-fifths Compromise did not deal with one of the following.

    a. counting slaves   c. representation
    b. taxation   d. treaty ratification

PROGRAMMED REVIEW

Knowledge Objective: To examine the major characteristics of democracy as a form of government

1. _____ is a system of government in which power is centralized in a few hands.

2. _____ is the term used to describe government by the many.
3. A representative democracy is commonly called a _____.

4. A constitutional government normally _____ the power of officials.

5. The central measure of value in a democracy is the _____.

6. The doctrine of _____ makes the community or state the measure of value.

7. _____ or _____ are terms used to describe the right of an individual to set his own goals.

8. In modern America the two major values that are in a state of tension and interaction are _____ and _____.

9. The basic democratic principle involved in elections is one person, _____ vote.

10. In democracies elections are decided by _____ vote.

11. To have a truly democratic election, citizens must have the right to _____.

Knowledge Objective: To analyze the structure of government under the Articles of Confederation and the events that lead to their abandonment

12. French revolutionaries of 1789 demanded the "rights of man"; American revolutionists demanded their rights as _____.

13. During the period 1781-89, Americans were governed under their first constitution, the _____.

14. Under the Articles of Confederation, a _____ was created rather than a national government.

15. The need to strengthen the machinery of government was demonstrated during the winter of 1786-87 by a debtor's protest known as _____.

Knowledge Objective: To discover how the Constitutional Convention of 1787 went about creating a "more perfect union"

16. The framers of the Constitution were guided chiefly by _____ rather than theory.

17. At the Constitutional Convention of 1787, _____ presided; _____ kept full notes; _____ was the highly respected elder statesman.

18. To encourage open discussion and compromise, proceedings of the Constitutional Convention were _____.

19. To break the deadlock over representation, the Connecticut Compromise provided that one house of Congress be based on _____; the other on _____.

20. The thesis that the founding fathers wrote the new Constitution primarily to protect their property rights was advanced by _____.

Knowledge Objective: To examine the political strategy that led to adoption of the new Constitution

21. Adoption of the new Constitution required ratification by _____ states.

22. Those who opposed adoption of the Constitution were called _____.

23. Hamilton, Jay, and Madison wrote a series of essays urging adoption of the Constitution that is known collectively as _____.

24. Opposition to the new Constitution was largely concentrated in the _____ region.

25. The strategy of those who favored adoption of the Constitution was _____.

POSTTEST

1. A democratic government is one in which all citizens have equal

   a. political influence.   c. social status.
   b. voting power.   d. economic benefits.

2. Believers in democracy do not accept

   a. statism.   c. individualism.
   b. equality.   d. liberty.

3. In modern America, two concepts once thought to be opposites exist in any uneasy relationship.

   a. equality and liberty   c. oligarchy and autocracy
   b. federal and unitary   d. socialism and capitalism
      government

4. Only one of these revolutionary leaders was present at the Constitutional Convention.

   a. Thomas Jefferson   c. Patrick Henry
   b. Sam Adams   d. Alexander Hamilton

5. The incident that did most to destroy faith in government under the Articles of Confederation was

   a. the Whiskey Rebellion.   c. the Loyalist revolt.
   b. Shays's Rebellion.   d. the Indian uprising.

6. The Founding Fathers favored all but one of the following ideas.

   a. a unicameral legislature   c. an independent judiciary
   b. a strong executive   d. a more powerful Congress

7. The Connecticut Compromise found a middle ground on the issue of

    a. representation.   c. the court system.
    b. slavery.   d. the electoral college.

8. The authors of The Federalist include all but one of the following.

    a. Hamilton   c. Madison
    b. Jefferson   d. Jay

9. To secure ratification, supporters of the Constitution promised

    a. presidential veto power. c. a federal income tax.
    b. a bill of rights.   d. a Homestead Act.

10. Only one of the following statements is true of the ratification
    process.

    a. The opponents tried to get   c. Most of the opponents were in
        a quick "no" vote.   rural areas.
    b. Most newspapers were   d. Opposition was concentrated in
        Federalist opponents.   the small states.

POLITICAL SCIENCE TODAY

1. Framing a Constitution Sir William Gladstone, the famous British
    Prime Minister, once described the American Constitution as "the
    greatest work that was ever struck off at a given time by the brain
    and purpose of man."
    Without detracting in any way from the Constitution-makers of 1787,
    how can it be argued that Americans were engaged in writing a
    constitution from 1607 to 1787? Can a case be made for the idea
    that the American Constitution is not yet written--although we have
    been engaged in that project from 1787 to the present date?

2. Constitutional Convention Organize the students into delegations
    to the Constitutional Convention (Virginia, Pennsylvania, New
    Jersey, South Carolina). For voting purposes, the first two can be
    considered as large states, the latter two as small states.
    Discuss and vote on the following proposals offered to the
    Convention:

    a. All adult males should be permitted to vote.
    b. The Convention should restrict its deliberations to revision of
        the Articles.
    c. The Congress shall consist of a single house.
    d. All states should have equal representation in the Congress.
    e. National taxes may be levied on the basis of the total
        population of a state.
    f. The right to import and own slaves shall be preserved forever.

g. Congress shall have unrestricted authority over foreign and interstate trade.
h. Congress shall choose the President.

KEY CONCEPTS

Differentiate: a. Constitutional republic and oligarchy
                   b. Direct democracy and a republic
                   c. Democracy and statism

Describe: How liberty and equality are interrelated

List: Four factors necessary for the democratic process

Explain: Why the American Revolution is considered conservative

Identify: Weaknesses of the Articles of Confederation

Indicate: At what point the framers of the Constitution
                   a. agreed   c. compromised
                   b. disagreed

Discuss: The motives of the founding fathers

Explain: The Federalist strategy to secure adoption of the Constitution

Analyze: The following quotations:
                   "A Republic . . . if you can keep it."
                   "We no longer sail upon a summer sea."
                   "The tree of liberty must be refreshed from time to time with . . . blood."

Explain: Why the bicentennial of our constitution is a truly remarkable occasion in the history of nations

ANSWERS

Pretest

1. a
2. a
3. b
4. a
5. a
6. d
7. d
8. a

9. c
10. d

Programmed Review

1. Oligarchy
2. democracy
3. republic
4. limits
5. individual
6. statism
7. liberty; freedom
8. liberty; equality
9. one
10. majority
11. organize
12. Englishmen
13. Articles of Confederation
14. league of friendship
15. Shays's Rebellion
16. experience
17. Washington; Madison; Franklin
18. kept secret
19. population; equality
20. Charles Beard
21. nine
22. Anti-Federalist
23. The Federalist
24. back country
25. quick ratification

Posttest

1. b
2. a
3. a
4. d
5. b
6. a
7. a
8. b
9. b
10. c

2 The Living Constitution

Although the framers of the Constitution wanted a strong government, they also feared concentrated political power. In this chapter we examine the restraints that were built into the Constitution (separation of powers, checks and balances, judicial review) and the flexibility our constitutional system has displayed in adjusting to changing conditions.

CHAPTER OUTLINE

   I.   CHECKS ON POWER
       A.   Division of power: between state and national governments (federalism)
       B.   Separation of powers: allocating national powers among the three branches of government
       C.   Checks and balances: shared powers, independent political bases, different terms of office, ambition against ambition
       D.   Judicial review: established by Marbury v. Madison

  II.   EVOLUTION OF THE CHECKS AND BALANCES SYSTEM
      The original checks and balances system has been modified by several political developments:
       A.   The rise of political parties
       B.   Changes in electoral methods
       C.   Creation of regulatory agencies
       D.   Changes in technology
       E.   The fact that the United States has become a world power

F. The expansion of presidential power
G. The contrasts between the American and the British systems

III. GROWTH OF THE CONSTITUTIONAL SYSTEM
    A. Congressional elaboration: structure of government and impeachment
    B. Presidential practices: center of American political system
    C. Judicial interpretation
    D. Constitutional flexibility: adaption to new conditions without amendment

IV. AMENDING THE CONSTITUTION
    A. Congressional initiative: proposed by two-thirds vote of each House, ratified by three-fourths of states
    B. National convention: amendments proposed by national convention, never used
    C. Results of the amendment process
    D. Ratification politics: ERA and D.C. Amendment

PRETEST

1. The branch of government most likely to dominate in the framers' opinion was the

    a. bureaucracy.   c. judicial.
    b. executive.   d. legislative.

2. The Nixon impeachment process is a good example of constitutional development by way of

    a. judicial review.   c. congressional elaboration.
    b. presidential practice.   d. custom and usage.

3. The presidential nominating convention is a good example of constitutional development by way of

    a. presidential practice.   c. custom and usage.
    b. congressional elaboration. d. judicial interpretation.

4. With one exception, ratification of constitutional amendments has been by action of

    a. the president.   c. state conventions.
    b. the Supreme Court.   d. state legislatures.

Match the items in the left column with the correct items from the right column.

5.	separation of powers	a.	based on custom
6.	checks and balances	b.	lame duck Congress
7.	shared powers	c.	allocates power among three branches
8.	<u>Marbury</u> v. <u>Madison</u>	d.	independent branches that are interdependent
9.	impeachment	e.	established principle of judicial review
10.	informal Constitution	f.	charges brought by House of Representatives
		g.	president signs congressional bill

PROGRAMMED REVIEW

<u>Knowledge Objective</u>: To analyze the original constitutional arrangements that diffused political power

1. In the United States, the symbol of national loyalty and unity has been the _____.

2. The constitutional arrangement that delegated certain powers to the national government and reserved the rest for the states is called _____.

3. The framers of the Constitution did not fully trust either _____ _____ or the _____.

4. The allocation of constitutional authority among three branches of the national government is known as _____ _____ _____.

5. The framers devised a system of shared power that is described by the term _____ _____ _____.

6. The varying terms of office for national officials were intended to prevent rapid changes by a popular _____.

7. In the United States the ultimate keeper of our constitutional conscience is the _____ _____.

8. The court case that established the practice of judicial review was _____ v. _____.

Knowledge Objective: To examine the developments that have modified the original checks and balances system

9. The president, Congress, and even judges have been drawn together in the American system by _____ _____.

10. Originally neither the _____ nor _____ were elected directly by the people.

11. Legislative, executive, and judicial functions are combined in some agencies, weakening the concept of _____ _____ _____.

12. In the modern United States, the branch of government that has acquired the greatest power is the _____.

13. The British system concentrates power and control in the _____ _____.

Knowledge Objective: To trace evolution of the Constitution by custom and interpretation

14. The customs, traditions, and rules that have evolved over the past two centuries are referred to as a(an) _____ Constitution.

15. The structure of the national judicial system was defined by action of _____.

16. The most discussed example of congressional elaboration of the Constitution during the Nixon years was the _____ process.

17. _____ age realities have increased the importance of the presidency.

18. The Constitution has been adapted to changing times largely through judicial _____.

Knowledge Objective: To analyze the amendment process and the constitutional changes made by it

19. To initiate a constitutional amendment requires a _____ vote by both houses of Congress.

20. Although it has never been used, an amendment can be proposed by a _____ _____.

21. A proposed amendment must be ratified in three-fourths of the states by either their _____ or _____ _____.

22. Congress (has, has not) proposed a great number of amendments.

Knowledge Objective: To examine politics of the amendment process in cases of ERA and the D.C. Amendments

23. In the case of _____ Congress altered the normal process by extending the time for ratification.

24. Equal Rights Amendment ratification has been blocked chiefly by a group of _____ states.

25. Opposition to the D.C. Amendment has come from _____ and _____ _____ districts.

POSTTEST

1. The framers of the Constitution depended heavily on one of the following assumptions about human behavior.

   a. Ambition will serve to check ambition.
   b. Most people want to do the right thing.
   c. Men are normally apathetic.
   d. Human savagery always lurks below the thin veneer of civilization.

2. The Founding Fathers created a system that

   a. encouraged participatory democracy.
   b. favored the popular majority.
   c. restricted decision making by popular majority.
   d. emphasized prompt, decisive government action.

3. The British democratic system differs from the American system in that

   a. the queen reigns but doesn't rule.
   b. Parliament has only one house.
   c. government authority is concentrated in Parliament.
   d. the High Court exercises judicial review.

4. The original checks and balances system has been modified by all but one of the following.

   a. the rise of political parties
   b. creation of regulatory agencies
   c. direct election of senators
   d. giving representatives a four-year term

5. As originally drafted, the Constitution was expected to

   a. cover all foreseeable situations.
   b. be a legal code, combining the framework of government and specific laws.
   c. be a general framework of government.
   d. be a philosophical statement of the relationships between individuals and society.

6. The Constitution of the United States has been altered without formal amendment by all but one of the following methods.

   a. congressional elaboration
   b. presidential practice
   c. custom and usage
   d. interposition by states

7. Compared to many state constitutions, the national constitution is more

   a. recent.
   b. complicated.
   c. specific.
   d. flexible.

8. The major tool of the courts in checking the power of other government branches has been

   a. impeachment.
   b. habeas corpus.
   c. judicial review.
   d. common law.

9. The constitutional arrangement that limits the power of American officials is known as

   a. separation of powers.
   b. prohibitions on authority.
   c. sharing of powers.
   d. implied powers.

10. During the Revolutionary period, legislatures

    a. were curbed by the checks and balances system.
    b. became the dominant branch of government.
    c. suffered from a steady decrease in power.
    d. governed firmly and wisely.

POLITICAL SCIENCE TODAY

1. Have all students read Article II, Section I, of the Constitution on the electoral college. Next have them read Amendment 12 to discover the changes of 1804.

   In duplicated form furnish students with three examples of the electoral vote, the popular vote, and the total electoral vote. For this purpose the results of 1948, 1960, and 1968 will be particularly pertinent. Next have students revise the vote of

14

these three presidential years, using alternate formulas described below:

Automatic Plan: This would eliminate the electoral college as such but would use the same formula for awarding a state's vote. While it would prevent "maverick" electors, it would change nothing else.

Run-off Plan: Retaining the electoral system, it would provide for a run-off election of the top two candidates, if no one gained a majority in the first election.

Proportional Plan: One version would apportion electoral votes in relation to popular vote. That is, if Democrats secured 60 percent of a state's vote, they would be given six of the state's ten electors, rather than all ten as at present.

Congressional District Plan: Electors would be elected by majority vote in Congressional districts. (Students will be unable to figure this exactly but should assume that the votes for electors would have been the same as that for the House.

Direct Popular Election: The total national vote would be used to determine the winner, without regard to district or state lines.

2. A critic of recent Supreme Court decisions involving the Constitution has written: "Today we live in perilous times, dominated by such doctrines as relativity. Our forefathers, the Founding Fathers, authored a great document, as valid for all time as the Ten Commandments. But modern judges, clever lawyers, have made of this rock of Gibraltar a weathervane, which swings to the prevailing political winds. Instead of the Old Constitution, which stood foresquare, they have constructed a barometer that rises and falls with every sentiment of the mob, every changing whim of the sociologists or psychologists. Modern Supreme Court justices make their decisions on precedent-setting decisions of their predecessors. What we need to do is get back to the original intention of the Founding Fathers. What was their plan? What did they want?"

If this idea of "original intent" were applied, what would be the result in cases involving affirmative action? Abortion? Capital punishment?

KEY CONCEPTS

Describe: The concepts of division and separation of powers. Include federalism and the distinctions between the three branches of government

Explain:	How the framers attempted to pit political ambition against political ambition
Differentiate:	Between judicial review and judicial interpretation
Discuss:	How the rise of political parties and technological development served to modify the checks and balances system
Identify:	The major differences between the British and the U.S. political systems
Indicate:	The evolution of the American constitutional system in the following areas: a. congressional elaboration b. presidential practices c. judicial interpretation
Explain:	The two methods for proposing constitutional amendments and the two ratification methods
Discuss:	The impeachment process outlined in the Constitution leaves little room for congressional interpretation. Agree or disagree.
Discuss:	Thomas Jefferson believed that every generation should write its own constitution. Agree or disagree.
Analyze:	a. Although the ERA Amendment had the support of dozens of strong interest groups, it was not adopted. Why? b. It is widely believed that the D.C. Amendment will fail. Why?

ANSWERS

Pretest

1. d
2. c
3. c
4. d
5. c
6. d
7. g
8. e
9. f
10. c

Programmed Review

1. Constitution
2. federalism
3. public officials; majority
4. separation of powers
5. checks and balances
6. majority
7. Supreme Court
8. Marbury v. Madison
9. political parties
10. president; senators
11. checks and balances
12. executive
13. legislative branch
14. informal
15. Congress
16. impeachment
17. nuclear
18. interpretation
19. two-thirds
20. constitutional convention
21. legislatures; ratifying conventions
22. has not
23. ERA
24. southern
25. rural; small town

Posttest

1. a
2. c
3. c
4. d
5. c
6. d
7. d
8. c
9. a
10. b

3

American Federalism: Problems and Prospects

The United States has a federal type of government, with power divided between the states and the nation. This division is spelled out in general terms in the Constitution. It is also an endless source of conflict. As this chapter demonstrates, a federal government is a good deal more complicated than one in which power is centralized or decentralized.

Federalism is more than a remote constitutional theory. It is also a day-by-day political issue involving money, influence, power, people. The various levels of government intermesh to provide a total government for Americans. In recent years the big debate has been over the disbursement of national funds to states and communities -- who gets what, when, where, how.

CHAPTER OUTLINE

    I. WHY FEDERALISM?
        A. Terminology: unitary, confederation, federal system
        B. Historical reasons: political climate, limited transportation and communication, agrarian society
        C. Political advantages: ease of expansion, unity without uniformity, innovation

II. CONSTITUTIONAL STRUCTURE OF FEDERALISM
    A. National powers: expressed, implied, inherent
    B. State powers: reserved, concurrent
    C. Constitutional limits and obligations at both levels
    D. Horizontal federalism: interstate relations (full faith and credit, privileges and immunities, extradition; interstate compacts)
    E. The realities of federalism today

III. TRIUMPH OF THE NATIONALIST INTERPRETATION
    A. Original states rights vs. nationalist position
    B. McCulloch v. Maryland: establishment of doctrine of national supremacy (implied powers)
    C. Growth of national government: war, commerce, taxation, general welfare powers

IV. UMPIRING THE FEDERAL SYSTEM
    A. Role of federal courts
    B. Other umpires and contestants

V. FEDERAL GRANT PROGRAMS
    A. Categorical
    B. Project
    C. Block
    D. Revenue-sharing
    E. The politics of federal grants
    F. Federalism and federal regulations
    G. Federalism: two levels or three?

VI. THE POLITICS OF FEDERALISM
    A. The politics of national growth
    B. The war among the states
    C. The future of the states

PRETEST

1. The best argument for retention of our federal system would be that it

    a. prevents the centralization   c. simplifies political party
        of power.   organization.
    b. provides cheap, efficient   d. provides both unity and
        government.   diversity.

2. The national government has all but one of the following powers.

    a. implied   c. reserved
    b. inherent   d. delegated

19

3. The state governments have only one of the following sets of powers.

   a. delegated and reserved   c. direct and inherent
   b. reserved and concurrent   d. expressed and implied

4. The states' rights interpretation of the Constitution conflicts with one of these concepts.

   a. broad construction   c. treaty among sovereign states
   b. reserved powers   d. state governments closer to people

5. The power of the national government that has not been a chief source of its expansion is

   a. to coin money.   c. to regulate interstate commerce.
   b. to declare war.   d. to levy taxes.

6. In the 1980s, one of the following best defines the power of the national government.

   a. all power specifically delegated by the Constitution   c. whatever needs to be done to promote the general welfare
   b. delegated powers plus powers implied from the delegated ones   d. dependent on which party is in power

7. In our history northerners, southerners, business people, and workers have

   a. consistently agreed on the role of the state governments.   c. changed sides in the debate over national-state powers.
   b. held to a single opinion with respect to national powers.   d. shown no discernible pattern of opinion at all.

8. Any group that "has the votes" in Washington is almost certain to favor

   a. a strong national government.   c. a Supreme Court critical of congressional power.
   b. states' rights.   d. local government as being closer to the people.

9. The great expansion of our grant-in-aid system occurred during

   a. the New Deal.
   b. the 1960s.
   c. World War I.
   d. World War II.

10. Current project grant programs are given out on the basis of

    a. total state population.
    b. individual applications.
    c. a percentage of minority citizens.
    d. a percentage of state contribution to federal revenues.

11. A federal grant that gives a state the right to spend money within a broad category is called a

    a. project grant.
    b. block grant.
    c. community action grant.
    d. grant-in-aid.

PROGRAMMED REVIEW

Knowledge Objective: To contrast federalism with alternate forms of government and to discover what advantages it offers Americans

1. A _____ government divides power between a central government and constituent governments.

2. The central government of a confederation exercises no power over _____.

3. A _____ government vests all power in the central government.

4. The relationship between American state and city governments is an example of the _____ form of government.

5. A federal government provides for _____ without uniformity.

6. Under our federal system such questions as divorce, gun control, and school dress codes are _____ issues.

7. The American people are most concerned with _____ politics.

8. Americans today (agree, disagree) _____ over the level of government that gives them the most for their tax dollars.

Knowledge Objective: To define how the Constitution allots power and the limitations it imposes

9. The Constitution delegates to Congress both _____ powers and _____ powers.

21

10. As an independent nation, the national government has certain _____ powers.

11. The powers shared by the national and state governments are called _____ powers.

12. The Constitution requires that the national government guarantee to every state a _____ form of government.

13. The _____ clause requires states to enforce civil judgments of other states.

14. The process by which a criminal is surrendered by one state to another is called _____.

15. A binding agreement among states that is approved by Congress is known as an _____ _____.

Knowledge Objective: To trace and explain the growth of the national government

16. Today Congress has the power to deal with (any, delegated) _____ issues.

17. The _____ interpretation of the Constitution argued that the national government was created by the states.

18. The nationalist interpretation of the Constitution argued that the national government was an agent of the _____ rather than the states.

19. The concept of implied powers for the national government was first established by the Supreme Court in _____ _____.

20. The Chief Justice of the Supreme Court who first set forth the doctrine of national supremacy was _____ _____.

21. The three major powers of Congress upon which national expansion is based are _____, _____, _____.

22. The umpire of the Federal system that has favored the national government is the _____ _____.

Knowledge Objective: To differentiate among the various types of federal grant programs and controls

23. _____ _____ grants involve matching federal-state funds for a specific program.

24. Local communities can receive federal funds directly outside any formula distribution under _____ grants.

25. Federal funds distributed according to formula for a broad purpose are called _____ grants.

26. The federal grant program phased out by the Reagan administration was _____ _____.

27. Federal regulations that bar state-local discrimination in employment are an example of _____ _____.

28. The national government has indirectly regulated automobile speed limits and minimum drinking ages through its financing of _____ construction.

29. Under the Reagan administration, national control of state and local governments (has, has not) _____ diminished significantly.

Knowledge Objective: To consider the relationship that has developed between national and urban governments

30. During the 1960s federal grant policy created a financial bond between the national government and _____.

31. Governors and state legislatures (do, do not) _____ like to have federal funds go directly to cities.

32. In recent years city officials have found state governments to be (more, less) _____ responsive to their problems.

33. _____ ideology normally favors state-local government.

34. From all political perspectives the prevailing mood today is one of (anti, pro) _____ Washington.

Knowledge Objective: To examine factors that have contributed to the expansion of the national government

35. The expansion of the national government can be explained in large part by our evolution from an agrarian society to an _____ society.

36. Our urban society has created a demand for programs operated by the _____ government.

37. Today many Americans identify closely with the national government because of their daily exposure to _____.

Knowledge Objective: To explore current developments that have changed the direction of federalism

38. The expansion of national grant programs has been curbed in recent years by budget _____.

39. Self-reliant governors who do not demand federal aid are largely found in _____ states.

40. In recent years sectionalism and regionalism among the states has (increased, diminished) _____.

41. In recent years the quality of state government has (improved, deteriorated) _____.

POSTTEST

1. The "states righters" basic premise is that the Constitution is a

   a. statement of principles.   c. treaty among sovereign states.
   b. union of people.   d. document inspired by God.

2. The basic nationalist premise is that the Constitution is a supreme law established by the

   a. people.   c. Creator.
   b. state.   d. Continental Congress.

3. Federalism can be defended in all but one of the following ways.

   a. Political experimentation   c. Allowances are made for
      is encouraged.   differences.
   b. Governed and governors are   d. A national majority can more
      in closer contact.   easily implement its program.

4. The supreme law of the land is composed of all but one of the following.

   a. the Supreme Court   c. U.S. law
   b. the U.S. Constitution   d. U.S. treaties

5. John Marshall's decision in <u>McCulloch</u> v. <u>Maryland</u> was that

   a. the government did not have   c. Scottish naturalized
      authority to operate a   immigrants can sit on the
      bank.   Supreme Court.
   b. state tax powers are   d. the national government has
      unlimited within their   the authority to carry out
      boundaries.   its powers in a variety of
                                        ways.

6. In interstate relations each state must accept without question one of the following.

    a. demand for extradition
    b. enforcement of civil judgment
    c. a Nevada divorce
    d. immediate voting rights for the other state's citizens

7. The average citizen of the United States today

    a. follows closely the activities of the state legislature.
    b. regards the citizens of other states as foreigners.
    c. is in close contact with local and state officials.
    d. is best informed about the national political scene.

8. Throughout our history, business had advocated

    a. states' rights.
    b. national supremacy.
    c. neither.
    d. both.

9. The present mood of the country with respect to federalism is best described as

    a. anti-Washington.
    b. pro city hall.
    c. less revenue-sharing.
    d. states' rights.

10. Under its partial preemption regulations the national government has sought to control

    a. surface mining.
    b. air quality standards.
    c. highway speed limits.
    d. occupational safety.

POLITICAL SCIENCE TODAY

1. Between 1980-1987 the national government eliminated revenue sharing with state and local governments. Interview the borough manager or county commissioner of your home community to discover what local programs had been partially funded from revenue sharing. Which of these programs have been continued? What new sources (if any) have been tapped? Has the total budget for the program been increased? Stabilized? Decreased? Eliminated? Has the elimination of federal funding resulted in political protests?

2. To test the relative importance of national, state, and local governments in the day-to-day lives of our people, have students conduct the following experiment:

    a. Listen to a fifteen-minute evening news program on radio or T.V. for five consecutive days. How much time is dedicated to the activities of each of these levels of government: (1) national, (2) state, (3) local?

b. Analyze the front page of a metropolitan newspaper for five consecutive days. How many column inches is given over to the activities of each of these levels of government: (1) national, (2) state, (3) local?

c. Conduct an information poll of ten college students, asking them to identify by name each of their national-state officials: (1) U.S. Senators (two), (2) U.S. Representative, (3) State Representative, (4) State Senator, (5) Members of U.S. Supreme Court (nine), (6) Members of State Supreme Court (as many as possible)

3. Have the class examine the thesis that the American Constitution has become sadly outdated by the march of events or that the original intentions of the Founding Fathers have been perverted by the Supreme Court. Organize the class into three or four major committees, each charged with the responsibility of reexamining and possibly rewriting a specific part of the Constitution in the light of these charges. Particular emphasis should be given to the possible reallocation of power between the national and state governments.

One committee might consider eliminating national regulations involving personal matters -- abortion, drinking age, seat belts; another might consider air pollution, water pollution, hazardous waste disposal; another might look at shifting most of the cost of education to the national government.

This is a tricky device that can get out of hand before the instructor realizes it, particularly if the activity gets bogged down in procedural matters. It does have the advantage, however, of involving each student in some hard thinking about the federal system and the nature of the society in which we live. The device not only permits an examination of the early Constitution framework, but places into focus the great changes that have occurred in our society since 1787. Rather than sweeping generalizations about such matters as states' rights, the student is faced with a series of specific issues in the federal structure.

Each committee should draft its recommendations, with majority and minority reports. These proposals can then be brought before the entire group for adoption or rejection. In this way every student is pushed toward a rethinking of the entire federal government.

KEY CONCEPTS

Differentiate: Confederation, unitary government, federal
                  government

List: Three major reasons that led the Founding Fathers
                  to adopt a federal system

Explain: The political advantages of federalism

Identify: One example of each of the following powers:
                  expressed, implied, inherent, reserved, concurrent

Discuss: a. The realities of federalism today
                  b. The necessity that the Supreme Court review
                      state laws
                  c. The belief that state governments are closer to
                      the people

Explain: The basic issue involved in the debate over
                  federalism

Describe: The current conflict between the Sun Belt and the
                  Frost Belt

Trace: The forces that led to an expansion of national
                  power

Differentiate: Among the major federal grant programs

Evaluate: The new controls over states using federal dollars

Discuss: a. "State governments today are providing
                      effective, responsive government."
                  b. "Before too long the only people interested in
                      state boundaries will be Rand-McNally."
                  c. "The expansion of direct federal aid has given
                      local governments unmistakable status as a
                      third component of the system."
                  d. "The good sense and practical judgment of
                      Americans (helps them) evade numberless
                      difficulties resulting from the Federal
                      Constitution."

ANSWERS

Pretest

1. d
2. c

3. b
4. a
5. a
6. c
7. c
8. d
9. b
10. b
11. b

Programmed Review

1. federal
2. individuals
3. unitary
4. unitary
5. unity
6. state
7. national
8. disagree
9. express; implied
10. inherent
11. concurrent
12. republican
13. full faith and credit
14. extradition
15. interstate compact
16. any
17. states' rights
18. people
19. McCulloch v. Maryland

20. John Marshall
21. war, commerce, tax
22. Supreme Court
23. categorical formula
24. project
25. block
26. revenue sharing
27. direct orders
28. highway
29. has not
30. cities
31. do not
32. more
33. conservative
34. anti
35. industrial
36. national
37. television
38. deficits
39. Sun Belt

40. diminished
41. improved

Posttest

1. d
2. a
3. d
4. a
5. d
6. b
7. d
8. d
9. a
10. c

4 First Amendment Rights

Almost everyone is in favor of freedom, but it is in the reality of social and political controversy that our basic principles are tested. In recent years the following issues, among many others, have been topics of disagreement and debate: church v. state; protected v. unprotected speech; freedom of expression v. executive privilege; obscenity v. community standards. In addition, numerous court cases have arisen over the right of people to assemble peaceably and to petition the government. Finally, there is the continual and perhaps inevitable problem of separating subversive and seditious from legitimate protest and free expression. This chapter examines each of these areas of controversy over freedom.

CHAPTER OUTLINE

   I.   INTRODUCTION
        A. Supports of a free society: freedom of speech, press, assembly, and petition
        B. The Bill of Rights: originally applied only to national government
        C. Civil liberties nationalized by "due process" clause of 14th amendment
            1. Gitlow v. New York (1925): First Amendment guarantee of freedom of speech protected from state action
            2. Subsequent Supreme Court decisions extended other provisions of the Bill of Rights

II. A WALL OF SEPARATION: ESTABLISHMENT CLAUSE ISSUES
    A. Freedom of religion
    B. Accommodationist - Nonpreferentialist Views
    C. The EStablishment Clause
    D. Applications
        1. Nativity scenes
        2. Devotional exercises
        3. Teaching of evolution
        4. Bible study
        5. Sunday closing laws
        6. Tax exemption of church property
        7. Aid to parochial schools
    E. Freedom of worship

III. FREE SPEECH AND FREE PEOPLE
    A. Permissible versus unconstitutional restraint on freedom of expression
    B. The need to distinguish among belief, speech, and action
    C. Distinguishing between protected and unprotected speech
        1. The bad-tendency doctrine
        2. The clear and present danger test
        3. The preferred position or absolutist doctrine
    D. Prior restraint, vagueness, overbreadth, least means, content neutral

IV. FREEDOM OF THE PRESS
    A. Right of access
    B. Freedom of information: sunshine laws, executive privilege
    C. Police searches
    D. Press coverage versus fair trials
    E. Student press rights
    F. Other means of communication: mail, motion pictures, television, radio, handbills, picketing, symbolic speech, commercial speech
    G. Libel, obscenity, pornography, fighting words

V. RIGHT OF THE PEOPLE PEACEABLY TO ASSEMBLE AND TO PETITION THE GOVERNMENT
    A. Freedom of association
    B. Subversive conduct and seditious speech
        1. Traitors, spies, saboteurs, revolutionaries
        2. Sedition speech: the Sedition Act, the Smith Act

PRETEST

1. Specifically, the Bill of Rights was aimed at

   a. the national government.
   b. the state governments.
   c. both national and state government.
   d. providing unlimited freedom to the people.

2. The due process clause, interpreted to mean that the states could not abridge the First Amendment freedoms, is part of the

   a. Fifteenth Amendment.
   b. Fourteenth Amendment.
   c. Eighteenth Amendment.
   d. Thirteenth Amendment.

3. Because of the Establishment Clause, states may not

   a. teach the Darwinian theory of evolution.
   b. study the Bible or religion in public schools.
   c. permit religious instructors to teach in public schools during the day.
   d. establish Blue Laws.

4. The Supreme Court has held that tax funds may not be used to

   a. furnish secular textbooks in parochial schools.
   b. furnish guidance and remedial help in parochial schools.
   c. pay fares to send children to church-operated schools.
   d. pay parochial teachers' salaries.

5. The doctrine that free speech cannot be restricted unless there is a close connection between a speech and illegal action is called

   a. the clear and present danger test.
   b. the speech and dangerous result test.
   c. the speech and action test.
   d. absolutist doctrine.

6. Of all forms of government interference with expression, judges are most suspicious of those that

   a. trespass on First Amendment freedoms.
   b. limit freedom of speech of any kind.
   c. impose prior restraints on publication.
   d. impose a posteriori restraints.

7. The current standards for obscenity are made

   a. by the Supreme Court.
   b. at the state level.
   c. at the community level.
   d. by Congress.

8. Persons may be convicted for one of the following.

   a. possessing obscene materials
   b. selling obscene literature
   c. importing obscene literature from abroad
   d. writing obscene material

9. Street marches by protest groups are protected by the First Amendment right to

   a. assemble.
   b. petition.
   c. demonstrate.
   d. boycott.

10. The formula which imposes on licensees the obligation to see that issues of public significance are covered adequately on radio and television is called

    a. equality doctrine.
    b. fairness doctrine.
    c. coverage doctrine.
    d. broadcasting code.

PROGRAMMED REVIEW

Knowledge Objective: To examine constitutional safeguards of freedom

1. The first ten amendments to the Constitution are known as _____ _____ _____.

2. The Bill of Rights originally limited only the _____ government.

3. The _____ _____ clause of the Fourteenth Amendment protects freedom of the press and of speech from impairment by the states.

Knowledge Objective: To inquire into the meaning of the wall of separation between church and state

4. The _____ clause is designed to prevent three main evils: sponsorship, financial support, and active involvement of the sovereign in religious activity.

5. Chief Justice Rehnquist has supported the _____ concept that government may support religion if they avoid favoritism.

6. The Court has held that a publicly sponsored Nativity scene (is, is not) _____ constitutional if the basic purpose is commercial.

7. Because of the Establishment Clause, states may not prohibit the teaching of Darwin's theory of _____.

8. The Supreme Court has ruled that tax funds (may, may not) _____ be used for teacher salaries and instructional materials in religious schools.

9. Sponsorship of prayer in school buildings by public school authorities (is, is not) _____ constitutional.

10. The Supreme Court (has, has not) _____ upheld the right of parents to deduct from their state taxes expenses incurred in sending children to public/private schools.

Knowledge Objective: To analyze the relationship between free speech and a free people

11. Government's constitutional power to regulate speech involves three forms: beliefs, speech, _____.

12. The limits of free speech were set forth as the _____ _____ _____ _____ test by Justice Holmes in Schneck v. United States.

13. The _____ position doctrine takes the view that freedom of expression has the highest priority.

14. Of all forms of governmental interference with expression, judges are most suspicious of those that impose _____ restraint on publication.

15. The Supreme Court (upheld, rejected) _____ efforts of the government to prevent publication of the Pentagon Papers.

Knowledge Objective: To investigate the scope of freedom of the press.

16. In a recent decision the Supreme Court (did, did not) _____ support barring of the press from a criminal case.

17. Congress (has, has not) _____ protected reporter notes from police seizure by restricting search warrants.

18. Supreme Court decisions (have, have not) _____ recognized a limited right of the President to withhold information under executive privilege.

19. Censorship of the mails is _____.

20. The _____ _____ _____ acts make most nonclassified records of federal agencies public.

21. Many states have passed so-called _____ laws requiring most public agencies to open their meetings to the public and the press.

34

22. Television (has, has not) _____ the same First Amendment rights as newspapers.

Knowledge Objective: To define limits on speech (libel, obscenity) that are constitutional

23. The First Amendment (does, does not) _____ prevent the FCC from refusing to renew a radio licence if in its opinion a broadcaster has not served the public interest.

24. The _____ doctrine imposes on broadcasters an obligation to see that issues of public significance reflect differing viewpoints.

25. The mere fact that a statement is wrong or even defamatory is not sufficient to sustain a charge of _____.

26. Under the current test a jury determines whether or not a work appeals to prurient interests or is patently offensive to _____ standards.

27. Obscenity (is, is not) _____ entitled to constitutional protection.

28. Dirty books and X rated movies are entitled to (less, the same) _____ protections as political speech.

29. The Attorney General's Commission on Pornography in 1986 found that there (was, was not) _____ a causal relationship between pornography and sexual violence.

30. Leadership in efforts to ban the sale of pornographic materials has come from _____ groups.

Knowledge Objective: To examine the right of the people peaceably to assemble and to petition the government

31. The right to assemble peaceably applies not only to meetings in private homes, but to gatherings held in _____ _____.

32. The right to assemble and to petition does not include the right to _____ on private property.

33. The rights of Iranian students in the United States and American Nazis to march on the streets (has, has not) _____ been upheld by the courts.

34. _____ consists only of the overt acts of giving aid and comfort to the enemies of the United States or levying war against it.

35

35. In the late eighteenth century the _____ Act made it a crime to utter false, scandalous, or malicious statements intended to bring the government or any of its officers into disrepute.

36. The first peacetime sedition law since 1798 was the _____ Act of 1940.

POSTTEST

1. Concerning free speech, Justice Holmes wrote that the best test of truth is the power of thought

   a. to endure over time.
   b. to be accepted by the majority.
   c. to get itself accepted in the competition of the market.
   d. to reflect the wisdom of the forefathers.

2. The bad tendency doctrine gives to _____ the power to decide what kinds of speech can be outlawed.

   a. courts
   b. legislatures
   c. the people
   d. local communities

3. Constitutional restrictions on establishment of religion include

   a. persons praying in school buildings.
   b. classes observing a moment of silence.
   c. public officials sponsoring prayer.
   d. studying the Bible.

4. The Freedom of Information Act of 1966 concerns

   a. censorship.
   b. press responsibility and fairness.
   c. abuses in the overclassification of documents.
   d. the right to privacy.

5. Legislation that would protect the confidential information of journalists from police and court investigations is called a _____ law.

   a. sunshine
   b. umbrella
   c. shield
   d. covert

6. In <u>Miller</u> v. <u>California</u> (1973), Chief Justice Burger defined obscenity as a work that

   a. lacks serious artistic, political, or scientific value.
   b. does not apply traditional standards of morality.
   c. is utterly without redeeming value.
   d. graphically describes sex relations.

7. The distribution of religious and political pamphlets, leaflets, and handbills to the public is

   a. constitutionally protected.
   b. under almost all circumstances locally prosecuted.
   c. constitutionally ignored.
   d. prohibited without a license.

8. Of the following, which has the greatest restrictions placed upon it by the Constitution.

   a. speech
   b. assembly
   c. picketing
   d. petitions

9. Persons may be restrained from assembling in

   a. any area designed to serve purposes other than demonstrations.
   b. courthouses.
   c. schools.
   d. privately owned shopping malls.

10. The Supreme Court decided that newspapers might publish a government study of our Vietnam involvement called the

   a. Five O'clock Follies.
   b. Pentagon Papers.
   c. Fire on the Lake.
   d. Red and Yellow; Black and White.

POLITICAL SCIENCE TODAY

1. <u>Pornography Ban</u> Using local or regional newspapers, identify a community that has attempted to regulate or outlaw pornography. What group or groups attempted to impose the ban? What criteria did they propose to screen the sale of material they believed to be pornographic? Did it extend to magazines? Books? Videocassettes? Movies? X-rated films?

   Which community group supported a ban? Which were opposed? What was the reaction of convenience stores? Bookstores? Adult movie operators? Video distributors? Public opinion?

Was the proposed ban adopted? Has it been enforced? Is the sale of pornography materials ever acceptable? If so, where?

2. <u>Libel</u> Select one of the following libel cases in <u>U. S. Reports</u>. State the facts in the case. Summarize the majority opinion. The dissenting opinions (if any). What precedent did this case establish?

<u>Near</u> v. <u>Minnesota</u> (1931)
<u>New York Times</u> v. <u>Sullivan</u> (1960)
<u>Curtis Publishing Company</u> v. <u>Wallace Butts</u> (1967)
<u>Associated Press</u> v. <u>Edwin A. Walker</u> (1967)
<u>George A. Rosenbloom</u> v. <u>Metromedia, Inc.</u> (1970)
<u>Elmer Gertz</u> v. <u>Robert Welch, Inc.</u> (1974)
<u>Time, Inc.</u> v. <u>Mary Alice Firestone</u> (1976)
<u>General Westmoreland</u> v. <u>CBS</u> (1984)
<u>General Sharon</u> v. <u>Time, Inc.</u> (1984)

KEY CONCEPTS

<u>Justify</u>:   The concept that ordinary citizens need a right-of-access to newspapers

<u>Define</u>:   The issues involved and the end result of <u>Muller</u> v. <u>Allen</u> (1983)

<u>Explain</u>:   The justification of a reporter's shield law

<u>Explain</u>:   How the Supreme Court brought state governments into compliance with the national Bill of Rights

<u>Describe</u>:   The three-part test created by the Supreme Court to determine if a statute violates the Establishment Clause (indicate what the Establishment Clause does and does not forbid)

<u>Illustrate</u>:   How the non-preferentialist view and the Establishment Clause may conflict

<u>Define</u>:   The Holmes-Brandeis clear and present danger formula (indicate what this formula requires in order to prosecute an offender)

<u>Explain</u>:   What the Pentagon Papers incident entailed

<u>List</u>:   The standards of obscenity as defined by the Miller decision

<u>Indicate</u>:   What the Fairness Doctrine requires

Explain: The Smith Act

ANSWERS

Pretest

1. a
2. b
3. c
4. d
5. a
6. c
7. c
8. c
9. a
10. b

Programmed Review

1. Bill of Rights
2. national
3. due process
4. Establishment
5. nonpreferentialist
6. is
7. evolution
8. may not
9. is not
10. has
11. action
12. clear and present danger
13. preferred
14. prior
15. rejected
16. did not
17. has
18. have
19. unconstitutional
20. Freedom of Information
21. sunshine
22. has not
23. does not
24. Fairness
25. libel
26. community
27. is not
28. less
29. was
30. feminist

31. public streets
32. trespass
33. has
34. treason
35. Sedition
36. Smith

Posttest

1. c
2. b
3. c
4. c
5. c
6. a
7. a
8. c
9. d
10. b

CHAPTER

5 Equal Rights under the Law

In a sense the Civil Rights movement began with the abolitionists prior to the Civil War. After the war the Thirteenth, Fourteenth, and Fifteenth Amendments which abolished slavery and established citizenship and voting rights were written into the Constitution. The "new" Civil Rights movement did not really begin until 1954 when the Supreme Court ruled that the separate-but-equal formula was unconstitutional. The 1960s saw additional and more improved civil rights legislation. In a continuation of its growth, civil rights legislation has been expanded and implemented by all branches of the government.

CHAPTER OUTLINE

I. TO SECURE EQUAL RIGHTS--AN OVERVIEW
    A. Concepts of equality
    B. Women's liberation
    C. The struggle for racial justice
        1. The national government begins to respond
        2. 1963: The turning point
        3. Black militancy, black awareness, and black power
        4. Two societies?
    D. Native Americans
    E. Hispanics
    F. Asians

II. EQUAL PROTECTION UNDER THE LAW--WHAT DOES IT MEAN?
   A. The rational basis test
   B. Suspect classifications
   C. Quasi-suspect classifications: sex and illegitimacy
   D. Is poverty a suspect classification?
   E. Age discrimination
   F. Fundamental rights
   G. How to prove discrimination

III. THE LIFE AND DEATH OF JIM CROW EDUCATION
   A. Is segregation discrimination? Plessy v. Ferguson
   B. The end of separate but equal: Brown v. Board of Education
   C. Busing and the federal courts

IV. BARRIERS TO VOTING
   A. Circumventing the Fourteenth and Fifteenth Amendments "legally"
   B. The National Government Acts
      1. Voting Rights Act (1965)
      2. Rise of black political power

V. BARRIERS TO PUBLIC ACCOMMODATIONS, JOBS, HOMES
   A. National powers to protect Civil Rights
   B. The Civil Rights Act of 1964
      1. Title II -- public accommodation
      2. Title VII -- employment
   C. The Civil Right Acts of 1866 and 1968: Fair Housing

VI. AFFIRMATIVE ACTION
   A. Government abandons neutrality
   B. The Bakke case
   C. Where do we stand

PRETEST

1. Since 1960 the women's movement has not concentrated on one of these issues.

   a. pay   c. parenthood
   b. pensions   d. peace

2. Only one of the following cities does not have a black mayor.

   a. Detroit   c. New York
   b. Los Angeles   d. Chicago

3. The civil rights gains of the 1960s chiefly benefitted

   a. young black males.   c. the black middle class.
   b. black welfare mothers.   d. poverty stricken blacks.

4. Major origins of Hispanics in the United States do not include

   a. Spain.   c. Puerto Rico.
   b. Cuba.   d. Mexico.

5. A state legislature may classify people only if the classification meets a _____ test.

   a. suspect   c. fundamental rights
   b. almost suspect   d. rational basis

6. In a famous dissenting opinion (Plessy v. Ferguson), Justice Harlan wrote

   a. most blacks are mentally   c. our Constitution is
      inferior.   colorblind.
   b. the black family must be   d. busing promotes tolerance.
      restructured.

7. One of the following is unconstitutional as an age classification.

   a. Driver licenses may not   c. A state policeman is retired
      be issued to those under   at age 55.
      16.   d. An applicant for a teaching
   b. A company's employees must   position (age 57) is rejected
      retire at age 70.   on the basis of age.

8. Slavery was abolished and black equal rights were granted by the _____ Amendments.

   a. Eighteenth, Nineteenth,   c. Sixteenth, Seventeenth, and
      and Twentieth   Eighteenth
   b. Thirteenth, Fourteenth,   d. Twelfth and Sixteenth
      and Fifteenth

9. In the 1930s, blacks resorted to which of these strategies to secure their rights.

   a. violence   c. litigation
   b. political power   d. persuasion

10. The civil rights movement produced its first charismatic leader, _____, during the Montgomery, Alabama, bus boycott of 1955.

    a. James Baldwin   c. Martin Luther King
    b. Dick Gregory   d. Jesse Jackson

PROGRAMMED REVIEW

Knowledge Objective: To examine the role of government in providing equal rights

1. Most of the equality debate in the United States is over equality of (opportunity, conditions) _____.

2. The American Dream has not emphasized equality of _____.

3. The focus of the modern women's rights movement has been to secure adoption of the _____ _____ Amendment.

4. The fastest growing minority in the United States is _____.

5. A top priority of Hispanics is _____ education.

6. The three largest subgroups of Hispanics in the United States are _____, _____, and _____.

7. Indian tribes are _____ of the nation, subject to supervision by _____.

8. After the Civil War, three "civil rights" amendments were added to the Constitution, the _____, _____, and _____ Amendments.

9. The first branch of the national government to become sensitized to the aspirations of black Americans was the _____.

10. In the 1930s, blacks resorted to _____ to secure their rights.

11. In the 1960s, the use of litigation by blacks was supplemented by a widespread _____, _____, and _____ movement.

12. The immediate origin of the black revolt occurred in 1955 when a _____ boycott was organized in Montgomery, Alabama.

13. The Kerner Commission concluded that the nation was moving toward two societies, one black, one white, and _____ and _____.

Knowledge Objective: To examine equal protection under the laws

14. The equal protection of the laws clause is part of the _____ Amendment and is implied in the due process clause of the _____ Amendment.

15. The Constitution forbids only _____ classification.

16. The traditional test of whether a law complies with the equal protection requirement is the _____ basis test.

17. Race and national origins are obviously _____ classifications.

18. The quasi-suspect classifications include _____ and _____.

19. Justice Brennan, speaking for the Supreme Court, declared that much past legislation placed women in a _____, rather than on a _____.

20. Poverty, according to the Supreme Court, (is, is not) _____ an unconstitutional classification.

21. Age (can, cannot) _____ be used as a criterion in employment if it is related to proper job performance.

Knowledge Objective: To describe the life and death of Jim Crow

22. In the 1954 case of _____ v. _____ the Supreme Court reversed its 1896 decision in Plessy v. Ferguson.

23. Segregation required by law is called _____ _____ segregation.

24. When segregation occurs without sanction of law, it is called _____ _____ segregation.

25. Busing across school district lines (is, is not) _____ required if the school district lines have been drawn to maintain segregation.

Knowledge Objective: To review barriers to voting

26. Most suffrage requirements, inside the U.S. constitutional framework, are fixed by the _____.

27. The Voting Rights Act of 1965 has been (effective, ineffective) _____.

28. The poll tax was abolished in federal elections by the _____ Amendment.

29. The Voting Rights Act of 1965 as amended set aside _____ tests throughout the country.

45

30. Black political power is (increased, diminished) _____ if elections are polarized around race.

Knowledge Objective: To examine racial and sexual barriers to public accommodations, jobs, and homes

31. Private clubs restricted to Italians are (constitutional, unconstitutional) _____.

32. The Fourteenth Amendment applies only to _____ action and not to private groups serving only their own members.

33. Segregation in places of _____ accommodation is unconstitutional.

34. A training program that gives preference to minorities or women (is, is not) _____ constitutional.

35. Persons who believe that they have been discriminated against may bring a _____ action on behalf of all of the people who have experienced similar discrimination.

36. Attempts through legislation to end housing discrimination (have, have not) _____ been a great success.

37. In the Bakke case the Supreme Court held that a special admissions category from which whites were excluded was (constitutional, unconstitutional) _____.

38. To redress the discrimination suffered by minorities, governments have adopted _____ _____ programs.

39. Affirmative action programs that give minorities special protection against layoffs are (constitutional, unconstitutional) _____.

40. Affirmative action programs may temporarily set _____ but not _____.

POSTTEST

1. Upon passage of the Nineteenth Amendment, women

   a. received equal pay.
   b. received equal rights.
   c. put an end to legal discrimination.
   d. got the right to vote.

2. Identify the unrelated word.

   a. freedom rides
   b. sit-ins
   c. bus boycott
   d. violence

46

3. The Kerner Report declared that

   a. violence is as American as apple pie.
   b. our nation is moving toward two societies, separate and unequal.
   c. affirmative action is un-American.
   d. black children should have neighborhood schools.

4. The fastest growing minority in the United States is

   a. Indians.
   b. Vietnamese.
   c. Hispanics.
   d. Blacks.

5. A reasonable government classification would be based on

   a. age.
   b. religion.
   c. sex.
   d. race.

6. Since 1960 the national government's role in the issue of equal rights has been

   a. to support discrimination.
   b. to remain neutral.
   c. to take affirmative action.
   d. to defer to the states.

7. One of the following situations is outside government jurisdiction.

   a. A restaurant bars men without jacket and tie.
   b. A hotel refuses to register a rock-and-roll star.
   c. A realtor refuses to sell property to an extended Vietnamese family.
   d. A theater refuses to seat a group with long hair and blue jeans.

8. One of the following is a fundamental right.

   a. travel
   b. housing
   c. welfare
   d. education

9. Which of these cases marked the end of the separate but equal interpretation of the Constitution?

   a. Plessy v. Ferguson
   b. Weber v. Kaiser
   c. Bakke v. California Regents
   d. Brown v. Board of Education

10. Which method used to prevent blacks from voting was outlawed by the Voting Rights Bill of 1965?

   a. literacy tests
   b. threats of violence
   c. poll taxes
   d. white primary

47

POLITICAL SCIENCE TODAY

Affirmative Action   Investigate your university's affirmative action
program. What proportion of the University faculty is women? Black?
Hispanic? Asiatic? How are these faculty members distributed among the
various academic ranks? Have there been any affirmative action
grievances? What is the situation in the non-teaching staff? What
about admissions? Are minorities actively recruited?

Since this may be a sensitive issue, the topic should be approached with
careful preliminary groundwork. Otherwise, investigating students may
walk into an extremely tense situation.

KEY CONCEPTS

Trace: The high points of the women's liberation movement
                  from the Civil War to ERA

Outline: The high points of the black struggle for equality
                  from Reconstruction to the present day

Discuss: The Kerner Commission conclusion: "Our nation is
                  moving toward two societies, one black, one white
                  -- separate and unequal"

Analyze: The demands of Hispanics, Indians, and ethnic
                  groups and their strategies to obtain equal rights

Describe: Suspect and quasi-suspect classifications, showing
                  how these have been used by the courts

Indicate: Why busing to achieve integration has become such a
                  confused issue

Examine: The effectiveness of the Voting Rights Act of 1965

Explain: Why government appears to have been more successful
                  in ending discrimination in public accommodations
                  than in housing

List: The areas of sex discrimination that have been
                  outlawed

Indicate: The actions taken by government to halt age
                  discrimination

Evaluate: The political clout of blacks in contemporary U.S.
                  politics

48

Analyze: The current status of affirmative action programs

ANSWERS

Pretest

1. c
2. c
3. c
4. a
5. d
6. c
7. d
8. b
9. c
10. c

Programmed Review

1. conditions
2. results
3. Equal Rights
4. Hispanic
5. bilingual
6. Mexicans, Puerto Ricans, Cubans
7. wards; Congress
8. 13th; 14th; 5th
9. presidency
10. litigation
11. social; economic; political
12. bus
13. separate; unequal
14. 14th; 5th
15. unreasonable
16. rational
17. suspect
18. sex; illegitimacy
19. cage; pedestal
20. is not
21. can
22. Brown v. Board of Education
23. de jure
24. de facto
25. is
26. states
27. effective
28. 24th
29. literacy
30. diminished

31. constitutional
32. government
33. public
34. is
35. class
36. have not
37. unconstitutional
38. affirmative action
39. unconstitutional
40. goals; quotas

Posttest

1. d
2. d
3. b
4. c
5. a
6. c
7. a
8. a
9. d
10. a

6 Rights to Life, Liberty, and Property

One of the hallmarks of the Anglo-American justice system is the
guarantee that a person is innocent until proven guilty. Persons
accused of crime have a great many protected rights: the right to
counsel; the right to be informed of the nature and cause of the
accusations; the right to a speedy and public trial; the right to be
confronted with hostile witnesses; protection against excessive fines;
and protection against cruel and unusual punishment.

Also, their property is protected against arbitrary government seizure,
and the government furnishes protection for property of the weak against
the strong.

CHAPTER OUTLINE

   I.   THE CONSTITUTION PROTECTS CITIZENSHIP
       A.   Basic rights protected under the Fourteenth Amendment (1868)
       B.   Citizenship: jus soli (place of birth) or jus sanguinis (by
           blood)
       C.   Loss of citizenship
       D.   Naturalized citizenship
       E.   Rights of American citizenship
           1.   State citizenship: residence v. legal domicile
           2.   National citizenship v. state citizenship
           3.   Right to travel abroad
       F.   Rights of aliens

1. First restrictions excluding certain undesirables (1875)
2. Limits on numbers and quota system (1924)
3. Current policy (quotas abolished) 1965, 1976, 1980 laws
4. Recent immigrant waves: Cubans, Mexicans, Vietnamese
5. Undocumented aliens: the Simpson-Mazzoli Bill

II. CONSTITUTIONAL PROTECTION OF PROPERTY
   A. Property rights v. individual rights
   B. Contract clause: states' powers to protect welfare restricted until 1880s
   C. 1934: contracts between individuals modified by state law
   D. Eminent domain

III. DUE PROCESS OF LAW
   A. Procedural
   B. Substantive

IV. FREEDOM FROM ARBITRARY ARREST, QUESTIONING, AND IMPRISONMENT
   A. Unreasonable search and seizure: definitions
      1. Exclusionary rule
      2. Third degree and the right to remain silent
      3. Right of privacy
      4. Writ of habeas corpus, ex post facto clause, bill of attainder
   B. Rights of persons accused of crimes
      1. Fourth, Fifth, Sixth, and Eighth Amendments
      2. Specific rights guaranteed: grand jury, counsel, speedy trial, impartial jury, right to have favorable witnesses and to confront adverse witnesses, prohibition against excessive bail
      3. Cruel and unusual punishment: capital punishment

V. NATIONALIZATION OF CIVIL RIGHTS
   A. Protection against double jeopardy
   B. Nationalization of due process: applying the Fourteenth Amendment to states
   C. Nationalization of equal protection laws
   D. Palko test: only rights implicit in concept of ordered liberty
   E. Doctrine of total incorporation

VI. HOW JUST IS OUR SYSTEM OF JUSTICE?
   A. Arguments against the system
   B. Arguments for the system

VII. THE SUPREME COURT AND CIVIL LIBERTIES

PRETEST

1. Identify the nationality not greatly involved in recent immigration.

   a. Italians
   b. Cubans
   c. Mexicans
   d. Salvadorans

2. Proposed reforms of existing immigration laws do not include

   a. deporting unmarried men.
   b. higher immigration quotas.
   c. giving permanent resident status to undocumented aliens.
   d. fining employers of undocumented aliens.

3. Conviction for one of the following actions has not been found to violate due process of law.

   a. treating the flag contemptuously
   b. to be on a public highway late at night without visible business
   c. to be a "common night walker"
   d. to carry a concealed pistol

4. Persons who are arrested by Federal officers at the scene of a crime are presumed to be

   a. guilty.
   b. innocent.
   c. accomplices.
   d. suspect.

5. Federally guaranteed rights include all of the following except

   a. no double jeopardy.
   b. application of ex post facto laws.
   c. excessive fines and unusual punishments.
   d. parole and/or probation.

6. The concept that private property cannot be taken for public use without just compensation is

   a. eminent domain.
   b. habeas corpus.
   c. ex post facto law.
   d. martial law.

7. Protection against self-incrimination should prevent

   a. double jeopardy.
   b. habeas corpus.
   c. eminent domain.
   d. the "third degree".

8. Aliens do not have the right to

   a. jury trial.   c. vote.
   b. freedom of religion.   d. attend school.

9. Faculty of state universities under the due process clause are guaranteed the right to

   a. tenure.   c. promotion.
   b. hearings before dismissal.   d. write uncensored books.

10. Substantive due process today is primarily concerned with

    a. property rights.   c. civil liberties.
    b. social policy.   d. economic regulation.

PROGRAMMED REVIEW

Knowledge Objective: To analyze how the Constitution protects citizenship

1. Citizenship was given constitutional protection in 1868 with the adoption of the _____ Amendment.

2. The principle of _____ _____ confers citizenship by place of birth.

3. The principle of _____ _____ confers citizenship by blood.

4. Under certain conditions naturalized citizenship may be revoked by a _____ _____.

5. Residence is primarily a question of (intent, physical presence) _____.

6. Privileges of state and national citizenship are (the same, different) _____.

7. Under existing practice an American citizen needs a _____ to enter or leave the United States.

8. Current immigration laws permit admission of 270,000 persons each year, with no more than 20,000 from _____ _____.

9. Current immigration law has permitted the admission of 150,000 refugees each year (inside, beyond) _____ the regular total.

10. Millions of illegal aliens have entered the United States from _____.

Knowledge Objective: To examine constitutional protections of property

11. The Supreme Court (has, has not) _____ held that contracts between individuals could be modified by state law.

12. The due process of law clause is contained in both the _____ and _____ Amendments.

13. There are two kinds of due process, _____ and _____.

14. Procedural due process (does, does not) _____ apply to many methods of law enforcement.

15. The unrestricted right of women to have an abortion during the first trimester of pregnancy is an example of _____ due process.

16. The Supreme Court (has, has not) ruled that state employees are not entitled to due process hearings before being fired.

17. A juvenile accused of delinquency must be guaranteed a hearing but is not entitled to having the decision made by a _____.

18. The state (may, may not) _____ refuse to pay the abortion expenses of poor women.

19. _____ due process places limits on how governmental power may be exercised.

20. _____ due process places limits on why governmental power may be exercised.

21. Substantive due process deals with the _____ of the law.

22. Since 1937, substantive due process has been revitalized as a limitation on governmental power in the field of _____ _____.

Knowledge Objective: To inquire into arbitrary arrest, questioning, and imprisonment

23. When in hot pursuit, the police (may, may not) _____ follow a person into his home and arrest him, even without a warrant.

24. Officers (may, may not) _____ stop and search suspects if they have reason to believe they are armed and dangerous.

25. A search warrant must describe what places are to be _____ and the things that are to be _____.

26. In <u>Mupp</u> v. <u>Ohio</u>, the Supreme Court ruled that evidence obtained unconstitutionally (can, cannot) _____ be used in a criminal trial.

27. Witnesses before a Congressional committee may not refuse to testify if they have been granted _____ .

28. Critics of the exclusionary rule argue that the solution is to punish the (police, suspect) _____ .

29. In <u>Miranda</u> v. <u>Arizona</u>, the Supreme Court held that a conviction (could, could not) _____ stand if evidence introduced at the trial was a result of "custodial interrogation".

30. A retroactive criminal law that works to the disadvantage of an individual is called an _____ _____ _____ law.

31. A legislative act inflicting punishment without judicial trial is called a _____ _____ _____ .

Knowledge Objective: To examine the nationalization of civil rights

32. Double jeopardy prevents two criminal trials by the _____ government for the same _____ offense.

33. The doctrine of "total incorporation" would make the due process clause of the Fourteenth Amendment a duplicate of the _____ _____ _____ .

34. The _____ test is a selective incorporation of fundamental rights within the Fourteenth Amendment.

Knowledge Objective: To evaluate our system of justice

35. Critics who claim our justice system is unreliable often point to trial by _____ as the chief source of trouble.

36. Critics charge that the grand jury has become a tool of the _____ .

37. Many members of minorities (do, do not) _____ believe that they have equal protection under the law.

38. In the United States, our emphasis on judicial protection of civil liberties focuses attention on the _____ _____ .

1. To become a citizen of the United States, aliens have to do all of the following things except

   a. renounce allegiance to their native country.
   b. swear that they will bear arms for the U.S.
   c. swear that they do not believe in world communism.
   d. own property worth at least $2000.

2. Naturalized citizens are not required to demonstrate that they

   a. are of good moral character.
   b. are able to speak and write English.
   c. know the principles of U.S. government.
   d. have a sponsoring family.

3. In its efforts to block the entry of illegal aliens, the Naturalization Service has been

   a. moderately successful.
   b. unsuccessful.
   c. extremely successful.
   d. uninvolved.

4. Juveniles and students are entitled to a jury trial before they are

   a. declared delinquent.
   b. sent to a mental hospital.
   c. suspended from school.
   d. sentenced for shoplifting.

5. Police do not have an unrestricted right to use

   a. trained dogs.
   b. secret cameras.
   c. recording devices.
   d. tapped telephones.

6. Only one of the following bugging situations is constitutional.

   a. foreign agents with presidential approval
   b. Mafia members by the FBI without a warrant
   c. counterfeiters by the Secret Service with Attorney General's approval
   d. business rival by his competitor

7. The "exclusionary rule" provides that certain evidence cannot be used to convict a person in a criminal trial.

   a. employees against employers
   b. children against parents
   c. illegal police searches
   d. testimony given in exchange for immunity

8. As a result of the Miranda decision, all persons accused of a crime have the following rights except

   a. to remain silent.
   b. have a lawyer represent them.
   c. freedom on bail.
   d. halt their interrogation at any point.

9. All of the following legal procedures are constitutional except

   a. habeas corpus.
   b. subpoenas.
   c. injunctions.
   d. bills of attainder.

10. The Palko test is best described as

   a. a medical test to determine drunkenness.
   b. a formula for applying the Bill of Rights to states.
   c. a criteria for determining the degree of murder.
   d. a test for naturalization.

POLITICAL SCIENCE TODAY

1. Civil Liberties   Interview a police officer, teacher, attorney, social worker, and a judge in your home community to get reactions to these questions:
   a. What standard procedures do police follow in making arrests and interrogating prisoners?
   b. How are prisoners informed of their rights?
   c. Are restrictions imposed by the courts a serious handicap in law enforcement?
   d. Are basic rights outlined in this chapter frequently violated in practice?
   e. What relationships exist between poverty, racial discrimination, unemployment, and crime?
   f. How does the school attempt to deal with incorrigible students? Are they successful?
   g. What kinds of procedures seem to work best in rehabilitating juveniles? First offenders? Repeaters?
   h. Is the family environment a major cause of criminal behavior?

2. Rights of Immigrants   Discover how many immigrants there are in the community.
   a. Do they get special financial assistance?
   b. Are they eligible for food stamps?
   c. Do the schools provide for special help?
   d. Who picks up medical bills?
   e. What kind of jobs do they fill? Do Americans suffer from unemployment as a result?

3. Immigration Trends

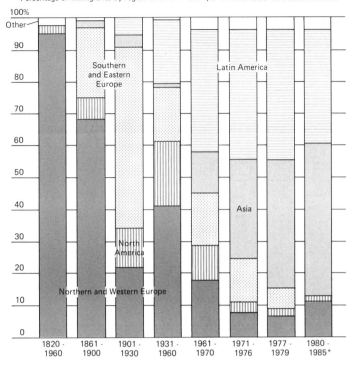

Percentage of immigrants by region of birth in each period. Numbers have been rounded.

*After 1979, figures for all of Europe are combined into one category

AMERICA'S CURRENT RACIAL MIX

Hispanic people can be of any race.
They make up 6.4 percent of the
population

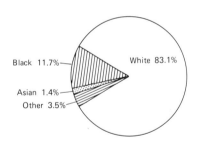

Black 11.7%

White 83.1%

Asian 1.4%

Other 3.5%

Prior to 1900, what region provided most U.S. immigrants? What
shift occurred in the period 1900-1960? What was the major source
between 1960-1976? What new region became the chief source after
1976?

In a book completed shortly before his death, Theodore H. White, a
lifelong observer of the American scene, raised a cry of alarm.
"Los Angeles," he wrote, "had ceased to be a city of European
culture. . . A new Athens might emerge or a new Calcutta." White,

59

quite obviously, feared that the answer would be "Calcutta". An economist, Phillip L. Martin, foresees a future America stratified by economic class, that is dominated by Anglos and Asians, while Hispanics and blacks are permanently relegated to a lower class.

Are these predictions overdrawn? What new problems do the immigrants create? What language crisis has been provoked by Hispanic immigrants? If current immigrant trends continue, what will the United States be like by the year 2050?

KEY CONCEPTS

Define:
The issues involved in coping with millions of illegal Mexican immigrants

Debate:
The "safe haven" versus the "protect American workers" attitude toward refugees

Describe:
The distinction between the Palko test and nationalization of the Bill of Rights

Discuss:
The rights of aliens as contrasted to those of American citizens

Explain:
The differences between procedural and substantive due process

Analyze:
By illustration and example both reasonable and unreasonable search and seizure

Discuss:
a. Advantages and disadvantages associated with protection against self-incrimination
b. The basis of support and opposition to the proposed immigration reform bill
c. The opposing arguments involved in charges of police brutality and the complaint that "a policeman's lot is not a happy one"

Evaluate:
Criticisms of the Miranda ruling

Debate:
The pros and cons of trial by jury

ANSWERS

Pretest

1. a
2. a

3. d
4. b
5. d
6. a
7. d
8. c
9. d
10. c

Programmed Review

1. Fourteenth
2. *jus soli*
3. *jus sanguinis*
4. court order
5. intent
6. different
7. passport
8. one nation
9. beyond
10. Mexico
11. has
12. Fifth; Fourteenth
13. procedural; substantive
14. does
15. substantive
16. has
17. jury
18. may
19. Procedural
20. Substantive
21. content
22. civil liberties
23. may
24. may
25. searched; seized
26. cannot
27. immunity
28. police
29. could not
30. ex post facto
31. bill of attainder
32. same: criminal
33. Bill of Rights
34. Palko
35. jury
36. prosecutor
37. do not
38. Supreme Court

Posttest

1. d
2. d
3. b
4. d
5. d
6. c
7. c
8. c
9. d
10. b

7 Interest Groups: The Politics of Faction

One permanent feature of our political landscape is the division of Americans into contending factions. Much of our political history can be captured in the rise and fall of these groups, their conflicts, and their compromises. Beyond their families, most Americans owe their top loyalty to an economic group, a professional group, an ideological group, and any one of hundreds of other causes that have their own group. James Madison foresaw and accepted this organization of society two centuries ago. Today interest groups seem to dominate the political scene far more than do political parties.

CHAPTER OUTLINE

I. THE MAZE OF INTEREST GROUPS
    A. Historical overview of factions
    B. The variety of interest groups

II. MAJOR INTEREST GROUPS: SIZE AND SCOPE
    A. Economic groups
    B. Non-occupational interest groups
    C. Political interest groups
    D. Foreign policy interest groups
    E. Single interest groups

III. FACTIONS IN ACTION
    A. Sources of power

B. Techniques: persuasion, elections, litigation, rule making
C. The growth of PACs
D. Lobbying: old and new approaches
    1. Old approaches: vote buying and bribery
    2. Modern, sophisticated lobbies
    3. Labor's political machine
    4. Cooperative lobbying

IV. CONTROLLING FACTIONS
    A. Spending regulations
    B. Lobbying as a moral issue: good or evil?

PRETEST

1. The loyalty of interest group members is often diminished by their

    a. overlapping allegiances.   c. limited time.
    b. inability to pay dues.   d. religious convictions.

2. Nearly all adult Americans belong to an _____ interest group.

    a. social   c. ideological
    b. religious   d. occupational

3. In recent years the great expansion of PACs has been in the _____ sector.

    a. labor   c. business
    b. professional   d. farming

4. The chief influence of PACs in election campaigns has been their

    a. contributions. c. door bell ringing.
    b. advice.   d. professional aid.

5. In their efforts to control factions and interest groups, the United States has rejected

    a. their prohibition.   c. regulating their activity.
    b. publicizing their activity. d. lobbying.

6. The American President who said that his experience in collegiate politics prepared him for a political career was

    a. Calvin Coolidge.   c. Lyndon Johnson.
    b. John Kennedy.   d. Ronald Reagan.

7. Which one of the following interest groups cuts across religious, ethnic, and economic groups?

    a. American Medical   c. Knights of Columbus
       Association   d. Young Americans for Freedom
    b. American Soybean
       Association

8. The interest group that has advocated an open political process and electoral reform is

    a. National Rifle Association.   c. Trilateral Commission.
    b. Nuclear Freeze.   d. Common Cause.

9. Efforts to represent the general welfare are thwarted by _____ groups.

    a. public interest   c. occupational
    b. single cause   d. organized

10. Labor's political clout is concentrated in a major PAC called

    a. CIO.   c. NIP.
    b. COPE.   d. POL.

PROGRAMMED REVIEW

Knowledge Objective: To examine factions as a force in politics

1. James Madison's famous essay on the role of factions is called _____ _____ _____.

2. Madison believed that popular government normally resulted in instability, injustice, and confusion because it encouraged the growth of _____.

3. Any group whose members share attitudes and try to achieve certain aims and objectives is called an _____ group.

Knowledge Objective: To describe the various kinds of interest groups

4. Nearly every employed person belongs to an _____ interest group.

5. The major farm interest group is _____ _____ _____; labor's largest group is _____; and the largest business group is _____ _____ _____ _____.

6. Common Cause is an example of a _____ _____ group.

65

7. The highly articulate spokesman for a conglomerate of consumer interest groups is _____ _____.

8. A prestigious foreign policy group, viewed with misgivings by both the Right and the Left, is the _____ Commission.

9. _____ _____ groups focus on highly specialized political issues.

Knowledge Objective: To investigate the techniques of interest group politics

10. Central tests of a group's power are its _____ and _____.

11. The cohesiveness of any interest group is weakened by _____ memberships.

12. Civil liberties, environmental, and black groups have used _____ as a weapon to achieve their goals.

13. The newest form of interest groups that back candidates and raise money are _____.

14. The great expansion of PACs during the 1980s was among _____ interest groups.

15. Contributors to PACs normally (do, do not) _____ demand immediate payoffs if their candidate wins.

16. The employee of an interest group who presents its point of view to legislators is called a _____.

17. Lobbyists have the _____ _____ needed by legislators for policy making.

18. Big labor's political arm is called _____.

19. Today it is not uncommon for U.S. House candidates to spend a _____ dollars.

20. Nearly _____ of all Congressional campaign funds come from PACs.

21. _____ is not a major criterion used by big corporations in financing the campaigns of Congressional candidates.

22. Most PAC funds go to _____ Congressmen.

23. The Food Group is an example of _____ lobbying.

24. _____ _____ people are underrepresented by interest groups.

25. The impact of the 1971 Federal Election Campaign Law has been to (increase, decrease) _____ the political activity of interest groups.

26. Interest groups provide _____ representation.

POSTTEST

1. James Madison urged the control of contending factions under the new constitution in an essay called

   a. Failing Factions.   c. Downing Number Nine.
   b. Letters of the Federal   d. Federalist Number Ten.
      Farmer.

2. Many of the strongest "unions" in terms of their political effectiveness are _____ organizations.

   a. recreational   c. feminine
   b. racial   d. professional

3. Those organizations that insist that they are solely devoted to the public welfare are called

   a. ideological.   c. public interest.
   b. professional.   d. political.

4. One of the following factors is normally not critical in determining a group's political strength.

   a. strong leadership   c. unity of membership
   b. size of membership   d. geographical distribution

5. Ralph Nader, the American Civil Liberties Union, and the NAACP have depended heavily upon _____ to influence public policy.

   a. litigation   c. persuasion
   b. direct action   d. campaign spending

6. The political arm of a business-labor-professional interest group is called a

   a. LEG.   c. CON.
   b. GYP.   d. PAC.

7. The least important factor in determining the support of candidates by business PACs is their

    a. voting record.   c. winability.
    b. incumbency.   d. party affiliation.

8. An interest group that "targets" political candidates on the basis of ideology is

    a. Americans for Democratic   c. AFL-CIO.
        Action.   d. COPE.
    b. National Education
        Association.

9. When a group finds the normal political processes closed, they are apt to turn to

    a. propaganda.   c. litigation.
    b. rule making.   d. persuasion.

10. From a Congressional point of view, the most useful service provided by lobbyists is

    a. public opinion polls.   c. influence.
    b. specialized information. d. speech writing.

POLITICAL SCIENCE TODAY

1. Interest Group Analysis Interview the responsible spokesperson for a national interest group that has a local unit in your home town. Prepare a written report covering these topics:
    a. What is the group's current legislative program?
    b. How does it raise its operating funds?
    c. How politically active are the members?
    d. What kind of two-way communication exists between leaders and members?

2. PAC Contributions Investigate total expenditures reported to the Federal Election Commission by the two major candidates in the last U.S. Senate race in your state. How much did each candidate spend? What percentage of the total was PAC money? Who were the major PAC contributors? Were these PACs locally based or national in scope? Repeat this investigation for the last House race in your district.

KEY CONCEPTS

Indicate: The most influential farm, labor, business and
                       professional interest groups

Analyze:	The reason that interest groups are so important in American politics
Discuss:	The special role played by public interest groups
Explain:	The factors that make an interest group politically potent
Describe:	The growth of PACs and their role in American politics
Discuss:	Proposals for controlling interest groups
Explain:	Results of the 1971 Federal Election Campaign Law
Analyze:	The techniques of interest groups

ANSWERS

Pretest

1. a
2. d
3. c
4. a
5. a
6. c
7. d
8. d
9. b
10. b

Programmed Review

1. Federalist No. 10
2. factions
3. interest
4. occupational
5. American Farm Bureau; AFL-CIO; U.S. Chamber of Commerce
6. public interest
7. Ralph Nader
8. Trilateral
9. single cause
10. size, unity
11. overlapping
12. litigation
13. PACs
14. business
15. do not

16. lobbyist
17. specialized knowledge
18. COPE
19. million
20. half
21. Party
22. incumbent
23. cooperative
24. low income
25. increase
26. functional

Posttest

1. d
2. d
3. c
4. b
5. a
6. d
7. d
8. a
9. c
10. b

8 Movements: The Politics of Conflict

In this chapter we turn to "movements", that, in contrast to groups, are organized outside the political system. In a general sense, movements press for sweeping changes in American values. Supporters of movements regard themselves as outsiders. They accept the necessity for direct action and conflict, while they try to gain majority support through public demonstrations.

Group politics is the politics of insiders. Movement politics is a challenge to the existing political system. For example, one anti-slavery leader, William Lloyd Garrison, called the Constitution "a covenant with death and an agreement with hell."

CHAPTER OUTLINE

    I.   WHY AND HOW OF MOVEMENTS
         A. Movements <u>vs.</u> Groups
         B. Characteristics of Groups
         C. Characteristics of Movements
         D. Examples of Movements
             1. Religious nonconformists
             2. Antitax
             3. Right wing

    II. MAJOR AMERICAN MOVEMENTS
         A. Blacks

        B. Women
        C. Indians
        D. Peace

   III. MOVEMENTS AND THE CONSTITUTION
        A. Not recognized originally
        B. Recognition won through evolutionary process

PRETEST

   1. Movements normally favor only one of the following political
       devices.

       a. grass roots political   c. lobbying
           action   d. compromise and consensus
       b. existing two-party system

   2. One of the following was not descriptive of Indian cultures.

       a. tribalism   c. patriarchal
       b. non-profit economy   d. communal

   3. One tactic was not commonly used by Blacks employing movement
       politics.

       a. legal challenges   c. sit-ins
       b. freedom rides   d. civil disobedience

   4. Early Black leaders who wished to improve the condition of freed
       slaves did not include

       a. W. E. B. DeBois.   c. Frederick Douglass.
       b. Ida Bell Wells-Barnett.   d. Angelina Grimke.

   5. One of the following women did not play a key role in the expansion
       of women's rights.

       a. Jane Eyre   c. Elizabeth Cady Stanton
       b. Lucretia Mott   d. Emma Willard

   6. The commonly accepted doctrine with respect to women's rights in
       colonial America was

       a. women had no rights before   c. spinsters are outside the law.
           marriage.   d. better an in-law than an
       b. a wife is dead in law.   out-law.

7. Identify the Black leader who is active today.

    a. Martin Luther King   c. Roy Wilkins
    b. Philip Randolph   d. Harold Washington

8. The chief concern of the Peace Movement today is

    a. nuclear weapons.   c. Pentagon waste.
    b. draft resistance.   d. veterans' benefits.

9. The most visible New Right movement today is called the

    a. Consumer Alert Council. c. Born Free.
    b. Moral Majority.   d. ERA.

10. A characteristic of movement politics includes a great emphasis on

    a. tactics.   c. elections.
    b. values.   d. lobbying.

PROGRAMMED REVIEW

Knowledge Objective: To analyze the characteristics of movement politics

  1. Movement politics tends to influence politics from the (inside, outside) _____.

  2. Movements normally arise when segments of the population find that the dominant political culture does not share their _____.

  3. Movement politics normally is successful in raising the political _____ of their followers.

Indicate the characteristic normally favored by movement politics in each of the following pairings.

  4. conflict vs. consensus _____
  5. lobbying vs. direct action _____
  6. public vs. private communication _____
  7. transactional vs. transformational change _____

Knowledge Objective: To examine movement politics as employed by the New Right, the antitaxers, and the nonconformist religious groups

  8. Nonconformist religious groups rejected _____ to preserve the State.

9. The antitax movement placed its major emphasis on cutting _____ taxes.

10. Popularity of the antitax movement resulted from a widespread distrust of political _____.

Knowledge Objective: To examine movement politics as employed by the New Right

11. The Conservative Caucus has mobilized a national membership through the use of _____ _____.

12. The chief spokesperson in opposition to ERA has been _____ _____.

13. President Reagan has been viewed by the New Right as a (steadfast, uncertain) _____ ally.

Knowledge Objective: To discover the nature of movement politics by tracing four major movements: Indians, Blacks, Women, Peace

14. All land in the New World originally belonged to the _____.

15. Many colonial claims to land ownership were based on _____ with Indians.

16. Clashes between white settler and Indians frequently resulted from a conflict of _____.

17. Chief Justice Marshall compared the legal relationship between Indians and whites as resembling that between a _____ and his _____.

18. In recent years Indians have asserted their tribal rights by _____ and _____ of ancient lands.

19. The central strategy question dividing the black community in its efforts to achieve equality has been whether to work _____ or _____ the federal system.

20. By the 1830s over a quarter-million persons protested slavery by joining the _____ Society.

21. The chief weapon used by the Ku Klux Klan to suppress blacks was _____.

22. In the 1950s segregated transportation facilities were challenged by CORE and SNCC through _____ _____.

23. Urban riots of the 1960s often began as black protests against _____ brutality.

24. In early American History women had no _____ rights.

25. The Nineteenth Amendment was a milestone in the women's movement that gave them the right to _____.

26. The slogan "59¢" came to stand for the _____ inequality between men and women doing the same job.

27. The original ERA Amendment failed because it was not approved by a sufficient number of _____ _____.

28. Today the general organization that promotes women's rights is _____.

29. The Peace Movement of the 1980s lacked (leadership, membership) _____.

30. A major factor in promoting the modern Peace Movement was the development of _____ weapons.

POSTTEST

1. Movement politics does not favor one of the following approaches.

   a. lobbying Congress
   b. raising political
      consciousness
   c. emphasizing an outsider role
   d. confrontation and conflict

2. U.S. Indian policy of the 1800s was based on the objective of

   a. ruling the tribes.
   b. absorbing them into
      American culture.
   c. regulating trade.
   d. ending tribal government.

3. Indians have recently had their greatest success in challenging the U.S. government by

   a. going on the warpath.
   b. movement militancy.
   c. getting out the vote.
   d. boycotting Congress.

4. The anti-slavery movement under William Lloyd Garrison favored which of the following policies.

   a. deportation to Africa
   b. freedom and U.S.
      citizenship
   c. placing freed Blacks on
      reservations
   d. intermarriage and affirmative
      action

75

5. Black movement politics did not include one of the following organizations.

    a. CORE   c. SCLC
    b. SNCC   d. NAACP

6. A study of the women's rights movement would suggest that

    a. your friends will help you   c. attach yourself to someone's
        out.   coattails.
    b. all things come in time.   d. the Lord helps those who help
                                          themselves.

7. The biggest problem faced by women in lobbying for ERA was the

    a. fragmented government   c. President Reagan's stand.
        system.   d. opposition men's groups.
    b. congressional opposition.

8. The Proposition 13 movement was concerned with

    a. affirmative action.   c. sexual harassment of women.
    b. Indian fishing rights.   d. reducing property taxes.

9. Movement groups tend to favor _____ change.

    a. incremental   c. transformational
    b. rational   d. no

10. New Right leadership has not been provided by one of the following persons.

    a. Richard Viguerie   c. Howard Phillips
    b. Phyllis Schlafly   d. Betty Friedan

POLITICAL SCIENCE TODAY

1. <u>Movement Politics</u> Prepare an analysis of one non-conformist religious group. Some groups worthy of study are the Amish, Mennonites, Black Muslims, Quakers, Doukhobors, Reformed Presbyterians, or the movement led by Jim Jones in Guyana. Among the questions your analysis should address are the following: What is the movement's attitude toward the existing political government? How large is the movement? What internal government does it have? Who has the leaders been? What was the source of their power? How was a sense of unity promoted? What relationship, if any, did it have with other parallel movements? What economic base does the movement have?

2. Comparable Worth   Title VII of the 1964 Civil Rights Act bans sex discrimination on the job.   Champions of women's rights have argued that this should be interpreted to mean that women get equal pay for jobs of comparable worth.   Several states (including Washington, Illinois, and Minnesota) have passed laws that implement that concept.   In a landmark decision of December, 1983, a Federal court accepted this interpretation and ordered Washington to give back pay and increases of $800 million to its 15,000 female workers.   If applied on a national scale, such a court ruling would be a fiscal revolution, since women workers earn only 60 percent of the wages paid to men.   Nor do they receive equal pay for comparable training and job assignments.

To check the validity of this charge, investigate the current salary schedule for non-academic employees on your campus.   Include the following groups.

Clerk-stenographer	Clerical supervisor
Fiscal assistant	Accountant
Electrician	Plumber
Yard worker	Nurse
Carpenter	Telephone operator
Security officer	Residence counselor
Secretary	Dining hall manager

Create two lists--one for jobs usually held by men; the other for women.   Using such criteria as skill, effort, responsibility, and working conditions, attempt to match jobs in one list with those in the other.   Do you discern any discrimination in current salary classifications?

KEY CONCEPTS

Analyze: The difference between movement and group politics

Describe: The characteristics that the Black, women, and Indian movements have in common.   What major differences exist between these movements?

Discuss: Why movements arise

Indicate: The scope of the New Right.   The relationship of movement politics and the Constitution

Analyze: How President Reagan defused the Peace Movement

Analyze: The success of New Right efforts to absorb religious fundamentalists

ANSWERS

Pretest

1. a
2. c
3. a
4. d
5. a
6. b
7. d
8. a
9. b
10. b

Programmed Review

1. outside
2. values
3. consciousness
4. conflict
5. direct action
6. public
7. transformational
8. violence
9. property
10. leadership
11. computerized mail
12. Phyllis Schafly
13. uncertain
14. Indians
15. treaties
16. cultures
17. ward; guardian
18. "fish-ins"; occupation
19. inside; outside
20. Anti-slavery
21. fear
22. Freedom Rides
23. police
24. legal
25. vote
26. salary
27. state legislatures
28. NOW
29. leadership
30. nuclear

Posttest

1. a
2. c
3. b
4. b
5. d
6. d
7. a
8. d
9. c
10. d

9 Parties: Decline and Renewal?

In this chapter we examine what political parties do and the causes of their decline in recent years. Political parties have many functions: simplifying choices, stimulating interest, recruiting leaders, aggregating interests, linking the mass public with government. Despite the importance of what they do, political parties seem to be declining. Numerous proposals are offered to strengthen our parties. These include procedural reform, broadening participation, changing delegate selection, and modernizing party policies and organization.

CHAPTER OUTLINE

    I.   BIRTH OF THE PARTY SYSTEM
         A. Party as the instrument of majority rule
         B. The rise and fall of partisanship
         C. Independent voters increasing
         D. Charges of party weakness

   II.   PARTIES: THEIR RISE AND THEIR ROLE
         A. The rise of the grand coalitions
         B. Key aspects of parties today
         C. No place for third parties?

  III.   PARTY FUNCTIONS: A HEAVY BURDEN

A. Historic function: to unify the electorate and conciliate groups.
B. Changes over time: public welfare becomes party concern
C. Party functions today: simplifying choices, stimulating interest, recruiting personnel, unifying groups, linking the mass public and government
D. Nominating candidates: caucus, convention, primary

IV. HOW THE PARTIES ARE ORGANIZED
A. Weakness at the top: the national committee and its chairperson
B. Parties at the grass roots: local committees lack organization, finance, and generally are inactive

V. ARE PARTIES WORTH SAVING?
A. Critics charge: lack of issues and weak organization
B. Tweedledum and Tweedledee?
1. Lack of issues, orientation overstated
2. Differences between party platforms significant
C. Parties in disarray
1. Weak party membership: professionals and amateurs
2. Variety of membership: strengths and handicaps
D. Parties vs. progress
1. Criticized for failing in times of rapid social change
2. Supporters assert decentralized parties are appropriate
3. Parties: growing and living institutions

VI. PARTIES TODAY: DEMOCRATS VS. REPUBLICANS
A. Issues and membership: sharp differences do not exist
B. Republican leadership: neoconservative
C. Democratic leadership: badly divided
D. Party strength and weaknesses

VI. SAVING THE PARTIES
A. Procedural reforms
1. Convention delegate selection
2. Party reorganization
B. Renewal
1. Democrats stress better party representation
2. Republicans stress new campaign techniques
C. Realignment
1. Party coalition building
2. Democrats under FDR
3. Republicans under Reagan
4. Future uncertainty

PRETEST

1. The Republican coalition put together by Ronald Reagan did not include

    a. born-again Christians.
    b. Blacks.
    c. white Southerners.
    d. conservatives.

2. Managing the presidential campaign is the job of

    a. the national committee.
    b. the national chairman.
    c. the attorney general.
    d. the presidential press secretary.

3. The first Republican party was led by

    a. Jefferson.
    b. Hamilton.
    c. Washington.
    d. Adams.

4. The more partisan a person is, the more likely he or she will look at his or her party's position with

    a. disregard.
    b. perceptual distortion.
    c. objectivity.
    d. evasion.

5. During the 1972 campaign, Richard Nixon depended largely on

    a. the Republican party.
    b. A personal organization called CREEP.
    c. television.
    d. personal popularity.

6. The purpose of a political party is

    a. to recruit potential officeholders.
    b. to simplify alternatives.
    c. to unite the electorate.
    d. all of these.

7. A striking characteristic of third parties is that

    a. they advance controversial issues and ideas.
    b. they are always radical.
    c. they are always conservative.
    d. they have no place in the American system.

8. The most significant factor influencing the character of American political parties is

    a. the federal system.
    b. the national convention.
    c. the party seniority system.
    d. the presidential primary.

9. Which of the following is not a present-day function of political parties?

a. distribution of welfare handouts

b. stimulation of interest in public affairs

c. recruitment of political leadership

d. linkage between the mass public and government

10. A major cause for the persistence of the two-party system in the United States is that

a. the major parties have become disciplined and issue-oriented.

b. election districts have a single incumbent.

c. third parties have failed to point up issues.

d. major party ideas and platforms are too much like religious dogma.

PROGRAMMED REVIEW

Knowledge Objective: To review the present state of our parties

1. The second U.S. constitution (unwritten) shifted power from the established branches of government to _____ _____.

2. During the past twenty years the number of _____ has grown rapidly.

3. Modern political parties have (more, less) _____ voice in choosing presidential candidates.

4. The Federalist party was challenged by the first _____ party, headed by Jefferson.

5. Today's _____ party (Grand Old Party) arose out of the Civil War.

6. _____ created a party coalition of Southerners, labor, farmers, the unemployed, and suburbanites.

7. _____ created a party coalition of business, "hard hats," Southern conservatives, and suburbanites.

8. Both parties today are (moderate, sharply different) _____ in policies and leadership.

9. Parties tend to _____ power that had been dispersed by the Constitution.

10. The American two-party system is maintained because in our single election districts only _____ candidate wins.

Knowledge Objective: To analyze party functions

11. Political parties formerly served as a kind of employment agency through their control of _____.

12. The Supreme Court has held that it is _____ to dismiss a public employee for partisan political reasons.

13. Party _____ include simplifying issues, stimulating interest, uniting different segments of society, and recruiting political leadership.

14. As a method of choosing candidates, the caucus was replaced by party _____ which on the state level were replaced by the _____.

15. The reason why political parties are so decentralized is the _____ basis of our government.

16. American political parties are basically loose _____ of state and local committees.

17. The supreme authority in both political parties is the national _____ convention.

18. A national _____ heads each of the two major parties.

19. Lacking organized party support in seeking nomination, a candidate builds a _____ organization.

20. Elections are regulated and run by _____, not the national government.

Knowledge objective: To look at the question, "Can parties be saved?"

21. The main charge against political parties is failure to take meaningful stands on _____ and weak _____.

22. The tendency to look at events through the eyes of a person's political party is called _____ perception or _____ distortion.

23. Recent scholars conclude that the Democratic and Republican parties are not _____ and _____.

24. The two types of members in our political parties are _____ or "regulars" and _____.

25. Parties appear to perform a "peacemaking" function best in time of _____ social change.

26. The forces for reform in the Democratic party were hotly opposed by more _____ Democrats.

27. Although Republicans and Democrats are not sharply divided along socioeconomic policy lines, they do differ markedly in _____.

28. Efforts to reshuffle existing political coalitions is called _____.

29. _____ have followed a middle path in their efforts at party reform.

30. Voters today describe themselves as more _____ than they did 20 years ago.

31. Republican efforts at party renewal have concentrated on more effective _____ techniques.

POSTTEST

1. Which of the following has almost doubled during the past decade?

   a. Democrats   c. independents
   b. Republicans   d. Socialists

2. The party that refused to face the issue of slavery and was replaced by the modern Republican party was

   a. the second Federalist c. the Whig party.
      party.   d. the second Republican party.
   b. the new Democratic party.

3. Third-party leaders have included all the following except

   a. John Anderson.   c. George Wallace.
   b. Barry Commoner.   d. Governor Jerry Brown.

4. In both major parties, the supreme authority is

   a. the candidate.   c. the national presidential
   b. the party chairman.   convention.
                             d. the primaries.

5. The grass roots of each party is

   a. in the Deep South.   c. at the city, town, ward, and
   b. in the western states.   precinct level.
                             d. at the family, church, and
                                school level.

6. The party that put together a grand coalition lasting from the Civil War until 1932 was

    a. Democratic.   c. Whigs.
    b. Republican.   d. none of these.

7. Street riots and other disturbances characterized the Democratic party convention in

    a. Kansas City, 1976.   c. Chicago, 1968.
    b. Atlantic City, 1964. d. New York, 1976.

8. The Democratic party has experimented with a variety of organizational reforms of which only one is currently operative.

    a. Southern regional primary   c. convention quota system
    b. midterm conference   d. enforced a unit rule

9. Republicans in the past decade have not emphasized one of the following reforms.

    a. membership recruitment   c. grassroots organization
    b. racial and sex quotas   d. candidate training programs

10. Both major political parties today are

    a. relatively weak.   c. class-oriented.
    b. strong coalitions.   d. tightly disciplined.

POLITICAL SCIENCE TODAY

Grassroots Political Organization Locate the local headquarters of a political party. Are these headquarters permanent or do they spring up only during an election year? What are the names of the state and national committee persons? Who heads the party at the county-city level? Interview at least one active member of the county committee. Query this individual on his or her views as to what the party stands for? Compare these views with those of national party leaders. Are they similar? Do differences exist? (To probe for similarities and differences, you must be prepared to ask specific questions on such issues as defense spending, welfare costs, abortion, school prayer, budget balancing, immigration restrictions.)

KEY CONCEPTS

Compare: The party coalitions put together by FDR, Nixon, and Reagan

<u>List</u>:	Republican party reforms under Bill Brock's leadership
<u>Discuss</u>:	The forces that cause the emergence of third parties
<u>Debate</u>:	Third parties are worth saving
<u>Explain</u>:	What is meant by a "grand coalition"
<u>Describe</u>:	The specific ways in which the two major parties differ
<u>Indicate</u>:	How and why American political parties are in trouble
<u>Explain</u>:	Why the United States has a two-party system
<u>Explain</u>:	What a regional primary is
<u>Describe</u>:	The reforms or changes attempted by the Democratic party commissions for the national nominating convention. What is their current status?
<u>Describe</u>:	The nature of Republican party renewal
<u>Describe</u>:	The socioeconomic background of Republican rank-and-filers as compared with Democratic rank-and-filers

ANSWERS

<u>Pretest</u>

1. b
2. b
3. a
4. b
5. b
6. d
7. a
8. a
9. a
10. b

<u>Programmed Review</u>

1. political parties
2. independents

3. less
4. Republican
5. Republican
6. FDR
7. Nixon
8. moderate
9. concentrate
10. one
11. patronage
12. unconstitutional
13. functions
14. conventions; primaries
15. federal
16. coalitions
17. presidential
18. committee
19. personal
20. states
21. issues; organization
22. selective; perceptual
23. Tweedledee; Tweedledum
24. professionals; volunteers
25. slow
26. centerist
27. leadership
28. realignment
29. Republicans
30. conservative
31. campaign

Posttest

1. c
2. c
3. d
4. c
5. c
6. b
7. c
8. a
9. b
10. a

10 Beliefs and Ballots: Public Opinion and Voting

Voting has always been somewhat of a mystery, but, thanks to recent research, we now know more about it. As this chapter shows, we have learned more about both voting and nonvoting, about the extent of political participation and the reason behind it. Perhaps the most important studies give us a better idea of how people make voting decisions and of the changes in voting patterns that are occurring in the 1980s.

Voting patterns to a great extent depend upon public opinion. A variety of forces help in the shaping of these opinions. Especially important is the intensity with which these opinions are held. Sophisticated polling now continually measures all aspects of public attitudes, including their intensity. As for voting, although nearly all adults now have a legal right to the ballot box, inequalities still exist because of race, sex and socioeconomic status. After the ballots are counted, the results are still open to varying interpretations, depending on the interpreter's bias.

CHAPTER OUTLINE

```
I.   POLITICAL SOCIALIZATION
     A.  The family
     B.  The schools
     C.  Other influences
```

II. THE FABRIC OF PUBLIC OPINION
    A. Surface v. fundamental forces
    B. Major characteristics: stability, fluidity, intensity, latency, salience, consensus, polarization

III. WHO VOTES? WHO DOES NOT?
    A. Causes of low turnout
    B. Who fails to vote
    C. Nonvoting: a critical problem?

IV. ELECTORAL PATTERNS
    A. Sectional; national
    B. Coattail effects
    C. Continuity
    D. Family
    E. Party loyalty
    F. Class, occupation, income
    G. Religion and race
    H. Gender; age
    I. Partisans and independents

V. TAKING THE PUBLIC PULSE
    A. Poll taking
    B. The tools of polling
    C. Difficulties of interpretation
    D. From opinions to votes

PRETEST
1. Nonvoters do not have one of the following characteristics.

    a. poor
    b. less educated
    c. less religious
    d. less white

2. Public opinion is best thought of as

    a. the will of the people.
    b. a diversity of opinion within a particular population.
    c. media reflection of public attitudes.
    d. voter attitudes.

3. An institutional barrier that blocks people from voting is

    a. distant voting booths.
    b. registration.
    c. unattractive candidates.
    d. lack of party competition.

4. The group least apt to vote is

    a. 18-24 year-olds.
    b. Gray Panthers.
    c. blue collar workers.
    d. women.

5. The most homogeneous of all groups in molding political opinions is

   a. school.   c. church membership.
   b. work.   d. family.

6. Which of the following was most apt to vote Democratic in recent elections?

   a. Jews   c. White Protestants
   b. Blacks   d. Catholics

7. The major force in the early socialization of children is

   a. TV.   c. the school.
   b. the family.   d. playmates.

8. The most influential factor in forming the attitudes of children is

   a. intelligence.   c. class and race.
   b. psychological and genetic   d. family and school.
      traits.

9. The most conservative economic attitudes are to be found in _____ homes.

   a. Catholic   c. atheist
   b. Jewish   d. Protestant

10. Younger voters with above-average incomes and college educations tend to be

   a. partisan.   c. independent.
   b. reluctant to vote.   d. Democrats.

PROGRAMMED REVIEW

Knowledge Objective: To examine how we acquire our political attitudes

1. The _____ unit instills the basic attitudes that shape future opinions.

2. The process by which we develop our political attitudes is called political _____.

3. The attitudes of children are shaped by their family and their political-social _____.

4. American schools tend to have an _____ point of view.

5. When a person's family background and peer group disagree, they experience _____.

6. Evangelicals tend to be (more, less) _____ socially conservative than nonevangicals.

Knowledge Objective: To consider the complexity of public opinion

7. The people speak with many voices. There is no one set _____ _____.

8. The characteristic of public opinion that causes it to change rapidly is called _____.

9. The characteristic of public opinion that does not change is called _____.

10. _____ attitudes are dormant but may be evoked into action.

11. Opinions which are closely associated with the lives of the individuals are called _____.

12. When a large majority of voters agree on an issue, we have reached _____.

13. When strong opinions are nearly equally divided on an issue, the result is _____.

Knowledge Objective: To identify those who vote and those who do not

14. In recent presidential elections, slight more than (half, three-quarters) _____ of potential voters cast ballots.

15. Compared to other nations, voting participation by Americans is (low, high) _____.

16. Millions of Americans fail to vote because they feel there is no real _____.

17. The key factor that determined the degree of voting participation is _____.

18. Persons in the 18-24 age group have the (highest, lowest) _____ voting participation record.

19. Highly educated people are (more, less) _____ apt to vote.

20. The paramount reasons for nonvoting are _____ and _____.

21. Institutional blocks are largely _____ and the _____ ballot requirements.

Knowledge Objective: To determine the patterns of American voting

22. Sectional patterns of voting tend to be (clear, fuzzy) _____.

23. Our national elections are frequently unpredictable because of the millions of _____ voters.

24. The _____ has the greatest influence in determining a person's voting patterns and party allegiance.

25. The best indicator of how a person will vote is _____ identification.

26. High income tends to be associated with the _____ party.

27. Nonvoting on the part of the _____ is a part of a larger political-psychological environment that discourages their political activity.

28. Women are more apt to vote for the _____ party.

29. The ability of a popular presidential candidate to help elect other candidates is called the _____ effect.

30. It seems that the religious cleavage in American politics continues to be (important, less important) _____.

31. More than a third of the voters can be called _____.

32. Blacks today are the strongest supporters of the _____ party.

33. Young voters (are, are not) _____ apt to be strong supporters of one political party.

Knowledge Objective: To examine the practice of "taking the pulse of the people"

34. An accurate poll must be based on a _____ sample of the total universe.

35. Samples based on a specific factor such as financial status are called _____ sampling.

36. One of the most successful types of questions asked by pollsters is in the form of the _____ choice question.

1. The most important factor underlying low Black voter turnout in the South is

   a. apathy.
   b. literacy tests.
   c. lack of organization.
   d. physical threats.

2. One of the following is not a reason why low-income people vote in fewer numbers.

   a. They have less sense of involvement and confidence.
   b. They feel at a disadvantage in social contacts.
   c. Their social norms tend to deemphasize politics.
   d. They can't afford registration fees.

3. All of the following are true about voter statistics except

   a. men outvote women by a large majority.
   b. middle-aged people are more likely to vote than younger people.
   c. college-educated persons vote more than high school graduates.
   d. persons who are active in organized groups are more likely to vote.

4. If one candidate is an especially able vote-getter, the party's whole slate may gain. This is called

   a. winner take all.
   b. the coattail effect.
   c. the domino effect.
   d. piggy-backing.

5. In off-year Congressional elections, the most important factor in determining voter behavior is

   a. party loyalty.
   b. economic well-being.
   c. candidate competence.
   d. Presidential support.

6. Historically, the Republican party has found its greatest strength in

   a. parts of the Midwest and New England.
   b. the South.
   c. the border states.
   d. the cities.

7. The group least apt to vote is

   a. Hispanics.
   b. Blacks.
   c. unmarried.
   d. Southerners.

8. An example of a universe in conducting polls would be

    a. a dozen students on the   c. voters in city X.
       Yale campus.   d. the man on the street.
    b. a Congressman's mail.

9. A good public opinion poll does not require

    a. qualified interviewers.   c. a 25% sample of the universe.
    b. carefully phrased questions. d. a representative sample of
       questions.   the universe.

10. Pollsters get the most accurate measure of public opinion through a
      _____ sample.

    a. representative   c. quota
    b. random   d. demographic

POLITICAL SCIENCE TODAY

1. Campus Profile Make a survey of the voting and political participation patterns on campus. How many students are registered? How many students voted in the last election? What is the political profile of the campus in terms of party identification? How does this pattern of party affiliation compare with the national patterns? Is the number of students who identify with the "Independent" status greater than the number of students who identify with the Democratic or Republican party?

2. Political Thermometer As explained in G. G. Henderson's An Introduction to Political Parties, the "Response" or "Feeling" thermometer offers an interesting exercise to test public opinion polling.

    Select one or two political figures who are well-known (Cuomo, Hart, Dole, Reagan) and poll twenty fellow students. For those who have no particular feeling toward the individual selected, mark the thermometer in the middle--50 degrees. Students with adverse, unfavorable feelings should rate the individual between 0 and 50 degrees. Those with favorable responses should rate the individual from 50 to 100 degrees. After two or more political figures are rated and compared, interviewees should be asked to account for their impressions. How much of this response can be attributed to the media? To television?

"Response" Thermometer

Warm $100°$ = very warm or favorable
           $85°$ = warm or favorable

```
        70°  =  fairly warm or favorable
        60°  =  a bit more warm or favorable
        50°  =  no feeling at all
        40°  =  a bit more cold or unfavorable
        30°  =  fairly cold or unfavorable
        15°  =  quite cold or unfavorable
Cold    0°   =  very cold or unfavorable
```

2. <u>Political Socialization</u> Prepare a self-analysis of your political attitudes and the sources from which they were derived. Begin with a personal profile that answers these questions.
   a. What political party do you favor?
   b. Are you a liberal, middle-of-the-roader, or conservative?
   c. What is your attitude toward government?
       1. Things are pretty good as they are.
       2. We need big changes.
       3. Things used to be better.
   d. What political party does your father favor? Your mother? Your community?
   e. To what income group does your family belong?
       1. $10,000-20,000
       2. $20,000-40,000
       3. $40,000-up
   f. Did you go to a public or private school?
   g. Which religious faith do you favor? Roman Catholic; Jewish; Fundamentalist Protestant; other Protestant; none?
   h. What is your racial-ethnic background?

If you have political attitudes that differ from those of your parents, what factors explain the difference?

KEY CONCEPTS

<u>Analyze</u>:   Why people fail to vote

<u>Describe</u>:   The categories that voters and nonvoters fall into

<u>Suggest</u>:   Ways in which the lower socioeconomic classes could be motivated to vote more (give some of your own suggestions)

<u>Analyze</u>:   What type of voter is likely to be an independent

<u>Discuss</u>:   Factors motivating people to become participants in politics

<u>Explain</u>:   Why there is no single political force that can be identified as public opinion

Indicate:	An example of saliency
Analyze:	The influence of the family, school, and church in formulating public opinion
Describe:	The importance of polling in the political process

ANSWERS

Pretest

1. c
2. b
3. b
4. a
5. d
6. b
7. b
8. d
9. d
10. c

Programmed Review

1. family
2. socialization
3. environment
4. Establishment
5. cross-pressure
6. more
7. public opinion
8. fluidity
9. stability
10. latent
11. salient
12. consensus
13. polarization
14. half
15. low
16. choice
17. education
18. lowest
19. more
20. institutional; political
21. registration; absentee
22. fuzzy
23. independent
24. family
25. party

26. Republican
27. poor
28. Democratic
29. coattail
30. important
31. independent
32. Democratic
33. are not
34. representative
35. quota
36. multiple

Posttest

1. c
2. d
3. a
4. b
5. b
6. a
7. a
8. c
9. c
10. a

11 Media Politics: The Blurred Lens?

Much of today's politics is played out before television cameras and watched nightly by millions of TV viewers as part of the six-o'clock news. The President is the focal point of this news, and anchorpersons are the stars in what seems to be an adversary relationship. Critics see the mass media as having almost unlimited power over public opinion, replacing the family, the community and political parties. This charge seems to be an overstatement, but the media does seem to be a central force in setting the national political agenda (the problems in the forefront of public discussion).

Most significantly, media dominance has greatly altered political campaigns. The great cost of recent contests is directly related to per minute charge for air time; voters seem increasingly to back candidates who have TV presence and charm.

CHAPTER OUTLINE

I. THE POWER OF THE MASS MEDIA
   A. Television focus on the President
   B. Concentration of media ownership
   C. Audience size and receptiveness
   D. The media impact on public opinion
   E. Setting the national agenda

II. MEDIA IMPACT
   A. Newspapers
   B. Television

III. THE MASS MEDIA IN ELECTIONS
   A. Media emphasis: personalities over issues
   B. The election as a game
   C. Campaign strategy: the media packagers
   D. Polling as a campaign technique

IV. EVALUATING MEDIA POWER
   A. Role of press in democracy
   B. The debate over media influence
   C. Rise of the national media
   D. Media bias?

PRETEST

1. Freedom of the press is guaranteed by

   a. American tradition.   c. Congress.
   b. common law.   d. a constitutional amendment.

2. One of the following media powers is normally not included in the top national ranking.

   a. Reader's Digest   c. Wall Street Journal
   b. ABC   d. USA Today

3. The news media exerts influence on the average voter by way of

   a. direct contact.   c. opinion leaders.
   b. political parties.   d. news broadcasts.

4. The network semi-monopoly over television has been _____ by C-SPAN and CNN.

   a. reinforced   c. untouched
   b. diminished   d. overshadowed

5. The media during a presidential election tends not to stress

   a. issues.   c. strategy.
   b. personalities.   d. the race.

6. Recent studies of the media's political reporting tend to be critical of their

   a. partisan bias.
   b. skimpy political coverage.
   c. repetitive coverage of issues.
   d. treatment of the election as a contest.

7. Among top newspapers, one of the following is not regarded as influential on national leaders.

   a. USA Today
   b. Washington Post
   c. Wall Street Journal
   d. New York Times

8. The number of people who watch television evening news is about _____ million.

   a. 1
   b. 20
   c. 30
   d. 60

9. The President who has been most successful in using television to further his goals has been

   a. Kennedy.
   b. Eisenhower.
   c. Franklin Roosevelt.
   d. Reagan.

10. The mass media's impact on most Americans is modified by their

   a. regionalism.
   b. viewing habits.
   c. lack of background.
   d. selective perception.

PROGRAMMED REVIEW

Knowledge Objective: To evaluate the power of the mass media

1. In modern America the mass media is so powerful that it is sometimes called the _____ _____ of government.

2. In financial terms the combined media has (more, less) _____ yearly revenue than IBM.

3. The privately-owned media enjoys special protection in the United States so that they can provide _____ in ideas.

4. Approximately _____ of the daily newspaper circulation is owned by twenty newspaper chains.

5. Most newspapers (do, do not) _____ have competitors in their local community.

6. Walter Lippmann called newspapers the _____ of democracy.

7. Political scientists have tended to (stress, play down) _____ the mass media's political influence.

8. Defense mechanisms such as _____ perception modify the influence of the mass media.

9. A powerful check on media as an opinion-making force is _____ _____.

10. Much of the media's opinion-making role is (direct, indirect) _____.

11. The final decision in determining the public agenda (is, is not) _____ made by the media.

Knowledge Objective: To investigate the media impact

12. President Nixon believed that the press was _____.

13. Modern presidents have turned away from the press and to _____ and _____ to communicate with the public.

14. In recent decades newspaper publishers tended to support _____ presidential candidates.

15. Generally, reporters are _____, while publishers take _____ positions.

16. Critics of presidential use of television have called TV an _____ _____.

17. The most influential part of the mass media is _____.

18. Members of Congress tend to be most concerned over the reporting of _____ television anchormen.

19. A recent study indicates that the liberal bias of reporters (is, is not) _____ reflected in their on-the-job performance.

Knowledge Objective: To evaluate the role of the media in elections

20. The media tend to portray the presidential election as a _____.

21. Public relations experts attached to campaigns tend to stress the candidate's _____.

22. Election experts tend to determine their campaign strategy on the basis of _____.

23. Old-time party leaders have been replaced in presidential campaigns by experts and _____.

24. A heavily-financed television campaign for the Democratic nomination of 1984 for _____ _____ failed.

Knowledge Objective: To evaluate media power in American politics

25. In evaluating media power, the media scholars (agree, disagree) _____.

26. Recent Presidential candidates have demonstrated their belief in media power by allocating at least _____ their budget to TV ads.

27. Most Americans believe that the media (is, is not) _____ a valuable watchdog over government.

28. The political topics that concern American voters (are, are not) _____ determined by the media.

29. Concentration of ownership among newspapers and TV has made the media (more, less) _____ partisan and critical.

30. The first concern of TV network owners is _____.

POSTTEST

1. In most national elections a majority of newspapers endorse _____ candidates.

   a. conservative
   b. liberal
   c. independent
   d. no

2. Critics of media employees charge that an overwhelming majority are

   a. conservative.
   b. liberal.
   c. independent.
   d. apolitical.

3. The most influential component of today's mass media is

   a. newspapers.
   b. television.
   c. radio.
   d. news magazines.

4. In addition to their public service role in providing information, the media also

   a. are privately owned.
   b. are big business.
   c. stress profits.
   d. are all of the above.

5. The modern President who has held the fewest news conferences has been

   a. Carter.
   b. Reagan.
   c. Ford.
   d. Johnson.

6. A member of Congress will be most concerned about news coverage by

   a. local TV news.
   b. national networks.
   c. C-SPAN.
   d. Washington Post.

7. Ownership of media outlets is

   a. widely dispersed.
   b. concentrated.
   c. unprofitable.
   d. family-oriented.

8. Political analysts originally underestimated the media's impact on public opinion because it did not have a _____ effect.

   a. emotional
   b. selective
   c. hypodermic
   d. psychological

9. The most adversarial relationship between the media and the President occurred during the _____ administration.

   a. Kennedy
   b. Johnson
   c. Nixon
   d. Carter

10. The public has the greatest confidence in

   a. news media.
   b. business.
   c. organized labor.
   d. government.

POLITICAL SCIENCE TODAY

Media Concentration and Major Newspapers

As the following tables show, concentration of ownership-control of U.S. newspapers continues to grow. A recent flurry of mergers has eliminated local ownership of nationally recognized newspapers in Baltimore and Louisville.

What are the basic forces that lie behind this trend? Why have most American cities ended up as "one-newspaper" towns? Are radio and television satisfactory alternatives to newspapers? What impact, if any, does this concentration have on American politics? What conclusion should be drawn from the fact that half of the top circulation newspapers in the United States have lost circulation in the past year?

NUMBER OF NEWSPAPER GROUPS AND DAILIES THEY CONTROL
(Selected Years, 1910 to 1985)

Year	Number of Groups	Number of Dailies	Percent of Total Dailies Group-Owned	Percent of Daily Circulation of Group-Owned Dailies
1910	13	62	--	--
1923	31	163	7.5	--
1930	65	311	16.0	43.4
1933	63	361	18.9	--
1935	59	329	18.9	--
1940	60	319	17.0	--
1945	76	388	21.0	42.0
1953	95	485	27.0	45.3
1960	109	662	31.3	46.1
1966	156	794	46.7	57.0
1970	157	879	50.3	63.0
1977	167	1,047	59.4	71.4
1978	167	1,095	62.5	72.2
1985	--	--	71.0	77.0

TOP 25 DAILY NEWSPAPERS

	Daily	Total Daily Circulation for 6 Mos. Ending March 31, 1986	Gain/Loss Over Same Period Last Year
1.	Wall Street Journal	1,985,559	-4,466
2.	New York Daily News	1,275,268	-115,687
3.	USA Today	1,168,222	+5,616
4.	Los Angeles Times	1,088,155	+18,591
5.	New York Times	1,035,426	+22,225
6.	Washington Post	781,371	+10,118
7.	Chicago Tribune	760,031	-15,633
8.	Detroit News	650,445	-16,031
9.	Detroit Free Press	645,266	-1,210
10.	Chicago Sun-Times	631,808	-7,379
11.	Long Island Newsday	582,388	+40,315
12.	San Francisco Chronicle	554,611	-368
13.	Boston Globe	514,097	+3,530
14.	Philadelphia Inquirer	492,374	-27,247
15.	Miami Herald	458,759	-5,986
16.	Cleveland Plain-Dealer	454,042	-10,209
17.	Newark Star Ledger	452,148	+17,344
18.	Houston Chronicle	425,434	-7,946
19.	Dallas Morning News	390,275	+21,592
20.	Minneapolis Star & Tribune	382,499	-1,158
21.	Boston Herald	358,725	-9,302
22.	Baltimore Sun	356,927	+7,026
23.	Portland Oregonian	335,162	+25,767
24.	Phoenix Arizona Republic	331,491	+5,814
25.	Denver Rocky Mountain News	320,441	-8,940

KEY CONCEPTS

Analyze: Reasons for the adversarial relationship that
                    normally develops between the media and the
                    President

List: Factors that tend to blur the media's impact on
                    public opinion

Explain: Why the media has great success in setting the
                    national agenda

Discuss: Concentration of media ownership tends to destroy
                    the original justification for protection of a free
                    press

Debate: a. Government-owned media would provide the public
                        with more and better information.
                    b. The media were an effective force in
                        challenging government policy in Vietnam and
                        Watergate.
                    c. TV anchorpersons are a political wild card --
                        unelected, irresponsible and powerful.

Analyze: a. The impact of television on the conduct of
                        presidential elections
                    b. Charges that television emphasizes
                        personalities and the "horse race" aspect of
                        elections over issues

Outline: Conflicting views of the mass media's influence

Review: The range of charges regarding the media's
                    partisanship and bias

ANSWERS

Pretest

  1. d
  2. a
  3. c
  4. b
  5. a
  6. d
  7. a
  8. d
  9. d
 10. d

Programmed Review

1. fourth branch
2. less
3. competition
4. half
5. do not
6. Bible
7. play down
8. selective
9. group affiliation
10. indirect
11. is
12. ultra-liberal
13. radio; television
14. Republican
15. liberal; conservative
16. electronic throne
17. television
18. local
19. is not
20. race
21. image
22. polls
23. consultants
24. John Glenn
25. disagree
26. half
27. is
28. are
29. less
30. profit

Posttest

1. a
2. b
3. b
4. d
5. b
6. a
7. b
8. c
9. c
10. a

12 Elections: The Democratic Struggle

Elections have always been somewhat of a mystery. However, in recent years, thanks to the research on voting behavior, we have greater understanding. We know, for example, that election mechanics--type and length of ballot, open or closed primary--have political consequences. This chapter explores the impact of the rules as well as the influences of political money. From here the discussion moves to running for Congress, the differences between campaigning for House and Senate, and the race for the biggest prize of all--the presidency. The final section deals with the mechanics and politics of the electoral college, the role of the mass media, and proposed reforms of the presidential primary system.

CHAPTER OUTLINE

    I.   THE CONSTITUTIONAL FRAMEWORK OF ELECTIONS
        A. The original pattern
        B. Modifications

   II.   RUNNING FOR CONGRESS TODAY
        A. Lack of competitiveness in House and impact of presidential elections
        B. Campaigning for the House: timing, visibility, personal organization, party support, personal contact
        C. Running for the Senate: big-time politics
            1. Cost, national issues, and campaign technology

2. Incumbency weighs heavily
3. Ride presidential coattails or disassociate?
4. Independent voters make campaigning more important

III. NOMINATING A PRESIDENT: PRECONVENTION CAMPAIGN, PRIMARIES AND CONVENTION
A. Choosing delegates: conventions and primaries
B. Types of presidential primaries
C. Presidential conventions: platform, nominating president and vice president

IV. THE FALL CAMPAIGN
A. Campaign strategy
B. Presidential debates
C. Electoral College system: mechanics and politics

V. CAMPAIGN STRATEGY AND FINANCE
A. Who gives and why
B. Campaign costs
C. Regulation of spending: 1971-1974 laws
D. Impact of campaign finance laws
E. PACs and congressional elections

VI. CRITICISM OF THE PRESIDENTIAL SELECTION SYSTEM
A. Pros and cons of primaries
B. Proposed reforms
C. Reforming the Electoral College
D. Analyzing recent elections (1980-1984)

VII. THE 1988 ELECTION
A. Roots in 1984 election: the Reagan coalition
B. The 1988 contestants

PRETEST

1. The most important factor in winning a congressional race is

a. personal contact.   c. press coverage.
b. TV time.   d. money.

2. Recent presidential conventions have been noteworthy because

a. the winner was known in   c. excitement ran high.
   advance.   d. philosophical differences were
b. major rivals made a down-   deep.
   to-the-wire finish.

3. The political strength of congressional incumbents has made modern elections

   a. highly competitive.   c. uncompetitive.
   b. political party contests.   d. strictly rational contests.

4. The campaign reform law of 1974 was chiefly concerned with

   a. campaign finance.   c. nomination procedures.
   b. media coverage.   d. delegate selection.

5. To attain the presidency, a candidate must achieve two goals. These are

   a. have the largest number of   c. be nominated at the party's
      delegates prior to coming   convention, and obtain both a
      to the national convention,   majority of the popular vote
      and then obtain a majority   and the electoral vote.
      of the popular vote.   d. be nominated at the party
   b. be nominated at the party   convention and win a majority
      convention, and obtain a   of the popular vote.
      majority of the electoral
      votes.

6. Black voters gave _____ percent of their support to Mondale in 1984.

   a. 50   c. 90
   b. 10   d. 30

7. In the opinion of observers, which of the following candidates gained votes for his ticket in the 1976 TV debates?

   a. Ford   c. Mondale
   b. Carter   d. Dole

8. In the event that no presidential candidate receives a majority of the electoral vote, the president is chosen by

   a. Congress.   c. House of Representatives.
   b. Supreme Court.   d. Senate.

9. In 1980 both Reagan and Carter received public subsidies for their campaigns of almost

   a. $5 million.   c. $15 million.
   b. $10 million.   d. $30 million.

10. The largest item in recent congressional campaigns has been for

    a. TV-radio advertising.   c. polls.
    b. consultants.   d. printing and mailing.

PROGRAMMED REVIEW

Knowledge Objective: To examine the process of running for Congress

1. Competitiveness in congressional elections (has, has not) _____ increased slightly over the past twenty years.

2. Senate elections are like to be (more, less) _____ competitive than House elections.

3. Congressional candidates whose vote is increased by a strong presidential candidate are said to benefit from the _____ influence.

4. New campaign technology tends to emphasize _____ over issues.

5. Keeping a House seat is (easier, harder) _____ than gaining one.

6. In midterm elections support for the party in power almost always _____.

7. We are probably entering a period in which campaigns will become (more, less) _____ significant in determining election outcomes.

8. Candidates for Congress secure most of their campaign funds from (the party, personal contributions) _____.

9. According to House Speaker Tip O'Neil, "all politics is _____ politics."

Knowledge Objective: To trace the steps in nominating and electing a president

10. Presidential candidates are now selected by their parties chiefly through the use of _____.

11. When voters in a presidential primary indicate their preference from a list of candidates, the election is commonly referred to as a _____ contest.

12. National conventions normally select a party candidate for president and vice president and write a _____.

13. The party platform is (binding, non-binding) _____ on the candidate.

14. Presidential candidate "bloopers" appear to have (little, great) _____ effect on the final vote.

15. To win the presidency, the candidate must have a majority vote of the _____ _____.

16. Under the electoral college system, a candidate either wins _____ or _____ of a state's electoral votes.

17. Most states provide for the selection of electors on a (state, district) _____ basis.

Knowledge Objective: To analyze the sources and uses of money in national campaigns

18. All congressional candidates (are, are not) _____ required to report their campaign contributions and expenditures.

19. Present federal financing of elections (does, does not) _____ give most of the money to political parties.

20. Federal financing of presidential elections has made it (easier, harder) _____ for rich candidates to win.

21. The key to congressional campaigns are _____.

22. Organizations and individuals (do, do not) _____ have limitations placed on the amount they may spend independently of a campaign organization.

23. Americans spend much _____ money per voter than do most countries on their elections.

24. Congressional candidates (do, do not) _____ receive federal campaign funds.

25. Reform of political money has pursued three basic strategies: limitations, disclosure, and government _____ for campaigns.

26. The 1974 campaign reform law achieved a breakthrough by providing for public _____ of presidential campaigns.

27. The Court has held that, if a party or candidate takes public funds, they can be required to _____ what they spend in the campaign.

28. The great bulk of private campaign money comes from _____, _____, and professional groups.

29. Major party candidates for the presidency now get _____ million in public funds to finance their general election campaigns.

30. Most money for the presidential election now comes from _____ sources.

31. Third party candidates (have, have not) _____ been encouraged by recent federal finance laws.

Knowledge Objective: To study proposed reforms of the electoral college and presidential primaries

32. Most criticism of presidential primaries suggests that they extend over too (long, short) _____ a period.

33. Reform of presidential primaries concentrates on _____ or a _____ primary.

34. Abolition of the electoral college seems to be a reform whose time (has, has not) _____ come.

Knowledge Objective: To define issues and personalities in the 1988 election

35. Nearly half (47% of eligible Americans (did, did not) _____ vote in the 1984 elections.

36. Looking ahead to the 1988 presidential election, (both, neither) _____ party has a candidate who is clearly a front-runner.

37. The dominant party at the state-local level is the _____ party.

38. Four of the last five presidential elections have been won by the _____ party.

39. The two major parties (did, did not) _____ have clearly contrasting attitudes on most national issues in 1988.

POSTTEST

1. Only one of the following presidential candidates was elected, although each received more popular votes than his opponent.

   a. Jackson (1824)   c. Tilden (1876)
   b. Cleveland (1888)   d. Truman (1948)

2. The bias of the electoral college favors

    a. one-party states.   c. populous urban states.
    b. rural areas.   d. modified one-party states.

3. A state's electoral vote is determined by

    a. population.   c. a complicated formula devised
    b. previous voting patterns   by Congress.
        in presidential elections.   d. the number of its
                                           representatives and senators.

4. The Supreme Court voided which of the following provisions of the
    1974 campaign reform law.

    a. limitations on spending   c. public funding of presidential
    b. limitations on giving   elections
                                       d. election-day registration

5. To be elected president, a candidate must receive

    a. a plurality of electoral   c. a majority of states as well
        votes.   as electoral votes.
    b. a majority of electoral   d. a majority of the popular
        votes.   vote.

6. Most delegates to the national nominating convention are chosen by

    a. popular votes.   c. state conventions.
    b. primary elections.   d. state committees.

7. Presidential candidates are nominated by

    a. party caucus.   c. national party committee.
    b. national party convention.   d. presidential primary.

8. New candidates for the House of Representatives are normally
    concerned with

    a. timing.   c. recognition.
    b. financial support.   d. all of the above.

9. The 1974 campaign expense law placed a limit on the contributions
    that could be made by

    a. individuals.   c. political parties.
    b. organizations.   d. all of the above.

10. The most important factor in President Reagan's 1984 victory was probably

   a. favorable economic conditions.
   b. his personality.
   c. the state of Soviet-U.S. relations.
   d. his concern for the poor.

POLITICAL SCIENCE TODAY

Tinkering With the Primary System Evaluate the variety of strategies now being used to increase the significance of state delegations to the national presidential conventions.
   a. Iowa caucus
   b. Michigan preprimary system
   c. Southern strategy (14 Southern states will have their delegate elections on the same day, March 8, 1988)
   d. California strategy (the largest single state delegation will be elected on the same day, March 8, 1988, as the Southern block vote
   e. New Hampshire strategy (the state has vowed to hold the earliest primary in the nation, whatever the date)

What were the 1988 results in Iowa? In Michigan? In the Southern states? In California? In New Hampshire? Did these results affect the party choice for 1988?

Evaluate each of the following proposals as to their impact on the presidential election process:
   a. Restrict state primaries to a time framework (5-10 months) before the election.
   b. A single national primary four months before the final election.
   c. A mini-convention 2 months before the November election dedicated only to writing party platforms.
   d. A general election in November with the winner being determined by the national popular vote.
   e. A general election in November with a winner in each Congressional district receiving one vote (plus two votes for carrying the state)

KEY CONCEPTS

Explain: Why contributions by "fat cats" have been relatively unimportant in recent elections

Describe: The strategies you would use to win a congressional seat

Identify:	The level at which recent presidential nominations have actually been won
Debate:	Whether the debates staged between presidential contenders have been useful to voters
Explain:	Why Congress has refused to provide federal financing for congressional elections
Analyze:	The impact of federal campaign finance laws on recent elections
Analyze:	The prevailing ideology of most major PAC groups
Analyze:	Criticisms of the electoral college system and the alleged advantages and disadvantages of various reform proposals

ANSWERS

Pretest

1. a
2. a
3. c
4. a
5. b
6. c
7. c
8. c
9. d
10. a

Programmed Review

1. has
2. more
3. coattail
4. personality
5. easier
6. declines
7. more
8. personal contributions
9. local
10. primaries
11. beauty
12. platform
13. non-binding
14. little

15. electoral college
16. all; none
17. state
18. are
19. does not
20. easier
21. PACs
22. do not
23. less
24. do not
25. subsidies
26. financing
27. limit
28. business; labor
29. thirty
30. government
31. have not
32. long
33. national; regional
34. has not
35. did not
36. neither
37. Democratic
38. Republican
39. did not

Posttest

1. d
2. c
3. d
4. a
5. b
6. b
7. b
8. d
9. d
10. a

13 Congress: The People's Branch?

To understand Congress, it is important to examine the characteristics of members of Congress, the impact of state districts and careerism, and the members' lawmaking representation roles. It is also necessary to understand the legislative "struggle," the unique nature of each house of Congress, and the manner in which Congress is attempting to resolve such questions as conflict of interest and the undue delegation of power. These are the topics of this chapter.

CHAPTER OUTLINE

    I. THE ROLE OF CONGRESS
        A. The first Congress
        B. Contradictory public views

   II. WHO ARE THE LEGISLATORS?
        A. Formal qualifications and typical backgrounds
        B. A profile of national legislators
        C. Historical evolution of congressional power
        D. Functions: lawmaking, consensus building, overseeing,
            policy clarification, legitimizing

  III. SAFE DISTRICTS AND CAREERISM
        A. Safe districts and reapportionment
        B. Advantages of incumbency

IV.   CONGRESSIONAL POWER
      A.   Formal constitutional powers
      B.   Special responsibilities of each house

 V.   JOB OF THE LEGISLATOR
      A.   Representation: delegate or trustee?
      B.   Influences on Congress: constituents, fellow members,
           ideology, congressional staff, lobbyists, political party,
           President
      C.   Obstacles to lawmaking

VI.   HOUSES OF CONGRESS
      A.   House of Representatives
           1.   Influence of the Speaker
           2.   Role of House Rules Committee
      B.   Senate
           1.   Majority leader's role
           2.   Folkways of the Senate
                a.   unlimited debate
                b.   the filibuster
                c.   club atmosphere
                d.   reciprocity

VII. COMMITTEES: THE LITTLE LEGISLATURES
      A.   The importance of committees
      B.   Major committees
      C.   Membership of committees
      D.   Chairmanship and staff control of committees
      E.   Seniority as a factor
      F.   Committee investigations: politics and information
      G.   Coordinating House-Senate committees
      H.   Distinguishing characteristics of each house

VIII. CRITICISM OF CONGRESS
      A.   Inefficiency: procedural road blocks, seniority, minority
           veto
      B.   Unrepresentative
      C.   Unethical
      D.   Irresponsible
      E.   Too much delegation of power: congressional staff,
           administrative agencies
      F.   Too much influenced by PACs

1. All of the following are true about senators and representatives
    except

    a. they come from upper and
        middle-class families.
    b. nearly half the members of
        Congress are lawyers.

    c. they are disproportionately
        from rural areas.
    d. a third come from blue collar
        occupations.

2. Gerrymandering occurs when the majority party

    a. supports benefits for blue
        collar workers.
    b. promises to promote
        legislation for certain
        districts.

    c. draws district lines to win as
        many districts as possible.
    d. draws district lines to
        maximize its popular vote.

3. The percentage of house members who are reelected is about

    a. 10.
    b. 50.

    c. 75.
    d. 90.

4. The chief responsibility of congressional staff is to

    a. handle constituent mail.
    b. serve as receptionists.

    c. schedule office appointments.
    d. advise on legislation.

5. Congress does not perform one of these functions.

    a. policy clarification
    b. consensus building

    c. foreign policy initiatives
    d. lawmaking

6. The Speaker of the House of Representatives does all of the
    following except

    a. grants recognition to a
        member.
    b. appoints select and
        and conference committees.

    c. controls committee
        assignments.
    d. directs general business on
        the floor.

7. In the Senate, the committee responsible for each party's overall
    legislative program is called the _____ committee.

    a. policy
    b. direction

    c. strategy
    d. ways-and-means

8. Legislators who base their votes on their analysis of the long-run welfare of the nation are playing a _____ role.

   a. delegate
   b. trustee
   c. pragmatic
   d. pollster's

9. Critics have complained that the seniority system has biased both houses toward

   a. liberalism.
   b. a "dictatorial" rule by the chairman.
   c. conservatism.
   d. do-nothingism.

10. Critics charge that Congress plays a brokerage role. This means

   a. moral decisions outweigh compromise.
   b. leaders bargain and negotiate.
   c. the majority dominates the minority.
   d. all members exercise options.

PROGRAMMED REVIEW

Knowledge Objective: To review the image of Congress in the public eye

1. The chief public complaints about Congress are that it is _____, _____, and not accountable enough.

2. Much of the ridicule of Congress is (justified, unjustified) _____.

3. Because of its dual roles, Congress has a _____ personality.

Knowledge Objective: To analyze the composition, attitudes, and career security of national legislators

4. The overwhelming number of national legislators are from _____ to _____ income backgrounds.

5. Nearly 50 percent of the legislators are _____ by profession.

6. _____ is the process of drawing electoral boundaries to maximize the majority party's house majority.

7. Redrawing the district lines of U.S. representatives after each census is the responsibility of _____ _____.

8. Being an incumbent is an (advantage, disadvantage) _____ for a member of Congress seeking reelection.

Knowledge Objective: To analyze the powers of Congress

9. The Senate has the power to _____ presidential nominations.

10. Members of Congress who see their role as _____ believe they should serve the "folks back home".

11. Members of Congress who see their role as _____ are free-thinking legislators who vote their conscience.

12. The main influence on legislators is their perception of how their _____ feel about the matters brought before Congress.

13. Most members of Congress are now highly dependent on their _____.

Knowledge Objective: To trace the lawmaking process

14. From the very beginning, Congress has been a system of multiple _____.

15. To follow a bill through the congressional labyrinth is to see the _____ of power in Congress.

16. Proponents of new legislation must win at every step; _____ need win only once.

Knowledge Objective: To analyze the structure of the houses of Congress

17. By sitting as the Committee of the _____, the House is able to operate more informally and expeditiously than under regular rules.

18. The Speaker of the House chairs the influential _____ _____ _____ Committee that was created in 1973.

19. Assisting each floor leader are the party _____ who serve as liaisons between the House leadership and the rank-and-file members.

20. In the Senate, each party has a _____ _____ which is in theory responsible for the party's overall legislative program.

21. By far the most important and enduring of the folkways in the Senate is _____.

22. Debate in the Senate can be shut off only by a _____ vote.

Knowledge Objective: To examine the committee system

23. All bills introduced in the House are sent to _____ committees.

24. As the power of Congressional subcommittees has expanded, the importance of _____ has diminished.

25. _____ are still usually named on the basis of seniority.

26. If neither house will accept the other's bills, a _____ _____ settles the difference.

Knowledge Objective: To examine major criticisms of Congress

27. Critics judge that Congress is _____ because the committee system responds too much to organized regional interests.

28. Congress lacks collective _____.

29. Congress (has, has not) _____ created Ethnics Committees to monitor the behavior of members.

30. There is a constant tendency for Congress to delegate authority to _____ agencies.

POSTTEST

1. The profile of a typical senator or representative would tend to bear out the charge that they

    a. are elitist.
    b. are ill-educated.
    c. are lower middle-class.
    d. overrepresent minorities.

2. Members of Congress from competitive districts are apt to make _____ their first priority.

    a. serving the home folks
    b. foreign policy
    c. national issues
    d. supporting the president

3. Special responsibilities of the Senate do not include two of the following.

    a. ratification of treaties
    b. confirmation of presidential nominees
    c. a final veto on appropriations
    d. nomination of ambassadors to foreign countries

4. In terms of the general makeup of Congress, which of the following people would be most typical?

    a. a millionaire Jewish stockbroker
    b. a Catholic steel worker
    c. a Protestant female elementary teacher
    d. a middle-income male lawyer

5. One of the following persons would have the best chance of election to Congress.

   a. an incumbent representative
   b. a popular TV anchorperson
   c. an experienced state legislator
   d. a famous woman astronaut

6. Free-thinking and independent legislators see their role as

   a. national figures.
   b. trustees.
   c. diplomats.
   d. ambassadors from localities.

7. The role of the president has become enhanced at the expense of the Congress, especially _____ policy.

   a. domestic
   b. foreign
   c. economic
   d. social

8. The vast majority of the 15,000 or so bills introduced every two years in both chambers are

   a. passed.
   b. still under debate.
   c. killed.
   e. withdrawn.

9. The majority floor leader is an officer

   a. only of his party.
   b. in charge of both parties in standing and conference committees.
   c. in charge of both parties on the floor.
   d. who presides over the Senate.

10. House party whips do all of the following except

   a. serve as liaison between leadership and the rank-and-file.
   b. inform members when important bills will be voted.
   c. lobby strongly for support of the majority leader.
   d. try to ensure maximum attendance for critical votes.

POLITICAL SCIENCE TODAY

1. Your U.S. Representative Prepare a check sheet on your U.S. Representative that provides this information:
   a. Congressional committees served on
   b. Location of district offices
   c. Bills introduced or sponsored
   d. Newsletter published? Frequency?
   e. Scheduled public meetings with constituents

f. Taped radio-television reports
g. PAC support in last election: Groups? Amount Contributed?
h. Visit the regional office to discover the number of personnel
    and the services they provide for constituents

2. Interest Group Evaluations Secure three current evaluations of
    your U.S. Representative and two Senators. Several major interest
    groups do this annually, e.g., Human Events, National Farmers
    Union, National Education Association. Congressional Quarterly
    each year summarizes the reports of the U.S. Chamber of Commerce,
    Consumer's Federation of America, COPE, AFL-CIO, Americans for
    Democratic Action, Americans for Conservative Action.

KEY CONCEPTS

Discuss: The major criticisms of Congress and proposals for
                  reform

Discuss: Confusion over the role of Congress

Discuss: The chief characteristics of the typical national
                  legislator (include changes under way in this
                  makeup)

Describe: The politics of reapportionment

Analyze: The consequences of incumbency on the makeup and
                  attitudes of Congress

Discuss: The role of the legislator as politician, committee
                  member, delegate and/or trustee

Explain: The types of pressures and influences a legislator
                  is subject to in decision-making or lawmaking roles

Analyze: The pathway of a bill through both houses (include
                  how and where it can be stopped)

ANSWERS

Pretest

1. d
2. c
3. d
4. d
5. c
6. c

7. a
8. b
9. c
10. b

Programmed Review

1. inefficient; unrepresentative
2. unjustified
3. split
4. middle; upper middle
5. lawyers
6. gerrymandering
7. state legislatures
8. advantage
9. confirm
10. delegate
11. trustee
12. constituents
13. staff
14. vetoes
15. dispersion
16. opponents
17. Whole
18. Steering and Policy
19. whips
20. policy committee
21. reciprocity
22. cloture
23. standing
24. seniority
25. chairpersons
26. conference committee
27. unrepresentative
28. responsibility
29. have
30. administrative

Posttest

1. a
2. a
3. c, d
4. d
5. a
6. b
7. b
8. c
9. a
10. c

14 The Presidency: Leadership Branch?

For the past generation, domestic and foreign crises have increased presidential power and responsibility. Additionally, there have been rising public expectations regarding strong presidential leadership. The result has been the emergence of the presidency as the leadership branch. Today, as we will see in this chapter, in spite of the "swelling" of the presidency and the Watergate scandals, the office still remains powerful, with great potential for leadership.

CHAPTER OUTLINE

   I.   THE EVOLVING PRESIDENCY
        A.   The framers' concept
        B.   Public expectations of the president
        C.   How strong a president?

  II.   THE PRESIDENT'S CONSTITUTIONAL POSITION
        A.   Intermingled powers of the three branches
        B.   Extension of presidential power limits
        C.   Congressional delegation of power: crises and war, domestic and economic problems, public expectations
        D.   Looking for leadership in the 1980s

 III.   THE JOB OF THE PRESIDENT
        A.   Crisis management
        B.   Symbolic-morale building leader

C. Recruiter-in-chief
D. Priority-setter, problem-clarifier
E. Coalition builder
F. Party leader

IV. THE PRESIDENTIAL ESTABLISHMENT
A. The executive office: the president's immediate staff
B. The Cabinet
C. The vice-presidency: White House puppet?
1. Duties mainly ceremonial
2. 22nd and 25th Amendments: a path to the presidency

V. MAKING THE PRESIDENCY SAFE FOR DEMOCRACY
A. The media role
B. Presidential character
C. New checks and balances
D. Public skepticism and expectations

PRETEST

1. Television does not make it possible for the president to

   a. talk directly to the   c. bypass the Washington press.
      people.   d. ignore public opinion.
   b. ignore Congress.

2. Critics of the presidency seldom charge that it is a _____
   institution.

   a. remote, aristocratic   c. status quo
   b. weak, flabby   d. Establishment

3. Only one of the following presidents is apt to appear on a list of
   "greats".

   a. Buchanan   c. Truman
   b. Grant   d. Harding

4. The framers of the Constitution did not anticipate presidential
   _____.

   a. symbolic functions   c. magisterial functions
   b. abuses of power   d. legislative role

5. The Supreme Court decision in Curtiss-Wright (1936) upheld strong
   presidential authority over

   a. foreign policy.   c. budget.
   b. domestic policy.   d. appointments.

6. The president's influence over his party includes selecting

    a. the party chairman.   c. state officials.
    b. congressional candidates. d. precinct workers.

7. The central presidential staff agency which advises the president about hundreds of government agencies is the

    a. Office of Oversight and   c. Office of Management and
       Investigation.   Budget.
    b. CIA.   d. GAO.

8. The vice president has not been used by modern presidents to

    a. chair advisory councils. c. undertake good will missions.
    b. execute day-to-day policy. d. serve as a senior advisor.

9. The Watergate experience seems to indicate that we should increase the power and effectiveness of all of the following except the

    a. vice president.   c. political parties.
    b. courts.   d. Congress.

10. The following persisting paradoxes of the American presidency are true except that a president should be

    a. programmatic, but a   c. a man who delivers more than
       pragmatic and flexible   he promises.
       leader.   d. above politics, yet a skilled
    b. a common man who can give   political coalition builder.
       an uncommon performance.

PROGRAMMED REVIEW

Knowledge Objective: To analyze the characteristics that Americans expect of their president

1. The framers of the Constitution wanted a strong leader but feared _____ of power.

2. The central characteristic that Americans demand of their president is the quality of _____.

3. In judging presidents, voters rate _____ and _____ over policy decisions.

4. The "electronic throne" from which modern presidents appeal to the people is _____.

Knowledge Objective: To examine the president's constitutional position

5. Rather than having a complete separation of powers, we actually have an _____ of powers.

6. The president's power is limited by a system of _____ and _____.

7. The dimensions of presidential power at any given moment are a consequence of the incumbent's _____ and _____.

8. During the past two centuries in democracies, power has shifted from legislators to _____.

Knowledge Objective: To analyze symbolic leadership

9. In accounting for the growth of the presidency, many blame _____ for delegating too much power.

10. The president has greatest inherent power in matters involving _____ affairs and national security.

11. The president's power has been greatly increased by the mass media, especially _____.

12. The swelling of the presidency in part results from the _____ expectations.

13. Presidents face a conflict between their role as chief of state and their role as _____ leader.

14. In acting for all of the people, the president is a symbolic leader and _____ of state.

Knowledge Objective: To examine the president's role as a recruiter and priority setter

15. The Supreme Court in the Curtiss-Wright case decided that the president (did, did not) _____ have exclusive powers in the field of international relations.

16. Since presidents appoint over 5000 top officials, one of the chief presidential duties is _____.

17. For economic policy the president depends on the Secretary of the Treasury, the Council of Economic Advisers, and the Director of the _____.

18. A president who is a successful leader knows where the _____ are.

19. To influence media coverage, the president holds _____ _____.

20. To gauge public opinion, presidents commission private _____
    _____.

21. Presidential candidates depend less on the organized _____ than on
    their personal political organization.

Knowledge Objective: To analyze the presidential establishment

22. In recent years presidents have come to rely heavily on their
    personal _____.

23. The office of _____ and _____ continues to be the central
    presidential staff agency.

24. Presidents seldom turn to the _____ as a collective body for
    advice.

25. The vice president serves as president of the _____.

26. The number of our presidents who were once vice presidents is
    approximately one-_____.

Knowledge Objective: To consider how to make the presidency safe for
democracy

27. The modern media is the Number One _____ of the presidency.

28. The American people regard television as (more, less) _____
    trustworthy than most other American institutions.

29. The theory which holds that a president in emergencies may act with
    discretion for the public good is called _____ theory.

30. James David Barber believes that we should pay more attention to a
    president's _____ than any other quality.

31. According to Barber, the people best suited for the presidency are
    _____ positive types.

32. To make the presidency safe for democracy, we should revitalize
    _____ _____ such as Congress, the courts, the press, and
    political parties.

POSTTEST

1. The American public today gives priority to one aspect of the president.

   a. leadership
   b. honesty
   c. wisdom
   d. policy positions

2. In the aftermath of Watergate, the public today favors

   a. a strong presidency.
   b. many more checks on the presidency.
   c. changing impeachment procedures.
   d. making Congress the dominant branch.

3. The trend in national policy making is towards greater

   a. centralization.
   b. decentralization.
   c. socialization.
   d. politicalization.

4. Presidents have the most leeway in

   a. foreign and military affairs.
   b. domestic appropriation matters.
   c. budget appropriations.
   d. social policy

5. Often a president's "new initiatives" in domestic policy are

   a. highly creative.
   b. previously considered in Congress.
   c. previously thought of by past presidents.
   d. a response to grassroots demands.

6. The functions of the White House staff include all but

   a. domestic policy.
   b. economic policy.
   c. congressional relations.
   d. intelligence operations.

7. If the president is to be a successful politician, he must be able to

   a. give commands.
   b. manage conflict.
   c. stand on principle.
   d. rise above politics.

8. Modern presidential cabinets as a collective body have been used by presidents

   a. as high-level advisers.
   b. to create a quasi-parliamentary system.
   c. very infrequently.
   d. to assess new policy proposals.

9. According to James David Barber, we should be most concerned with a presidential candidate's

   a. stand on the issues.
   b. knowledge and past political experiences.
   c. character.
   d. television image.

10. According to Barber, the worst type of presidential character is

   a. active-positive.
   b. active-negative.
   c. passive-positive.
   d. passive-negative.

POLITICAL SCIENCE TODAY

1. A Failed Presidency Most emphasis tends to center on great or near-great presidents. Perhaps as much can be learned by examining in some depth the administration of a "failed" president--one whom historians judge not to have measured up to the office. Among frequently mentioned presidents in this category are: Buchanan, Grant, Coolidge, Hoover, and Harding.

   Examine the presidential career of one of these presidents. What personal flaws seemed to handicap his administration? Did he have bad advisors? What major mistakes did he make? Why was he originally selected? Could he have succeeded under different circumstances?

2. Reagan's Successor Commonly it is asserted that no one can successfully follow Ronald Reagan--that his great communication skills, ingratiating manner, ability to work with Congress, and his tough stance in foreign relations cannot be duplicated.

   Yet we will have another president on January 20, 1989. Assuming you are elected as his successor, what public image would you adopt? Draft a profile of an ideal successor. Would you try to imitate Reagan? Stress differences? Try to avoid comparisons? Change the pattern of White House life? Hold more press conferences? Fewer? More TV appearances? Emphasize your unique strengths?

KEY CONCEPTS

Debate: Whose concept of the presidency prevails today: Jefferson or Adams?

Justify: Why the power to persuade is more important than the power to command in the presidency

Illustrate: How the president can reach the people, and why public opinion is so important

Outline: The principle offices and roles of the executive office of the president

Indicate: The functions of the White House Office and who comprises it

Explain: The factors that have increased presidential power (include Congress, crises, television, and federal programs)

Illustrate: How the president is a symbolic leader

Define: What is meant by Barber's active-positive presidential character type

Resolve: (If you can) the paradoxes of public expectations for the presidency

Discuss: a. "The media destroy every hero . . . they strip them naked."
                            b. ". . . if it were left to me to decide whether we should have a government without newspapers or newspapers without a government, I prefer the latter."

ANSWERS

Pretest

1. d
2. b
3. c
4. a
5. a
6. a
7. c
8. b
9. a

10. c

Programmed Review

1. abuses
2. leadership
3. character; integrity
4. television
5. intermingling
6. checks and balances
7. character; energy
8. executives
9. Congress
10. foreign
11. television
12. public's
13. party
14. chief
15. did
16. recruitment
17. OBM
18. followers
19. press conferences
20. opinion polls
21. party
22. staff
23. Management; Budget
24. Cabinet
25. Senate
26. third
27. adversary
28. more
29. prerogative
30. character
31. active
32. auxiliary precautions

Posttest

1. a
2. a
3. a
4. a
5. b
6. d
7. b
8. c
9. c
10. b

15 Congress v. President: The Politics of Shared Powers

In reviewing congressional-presidential relations, we consider the impact of Watergate, the imperial presidency, the practice of impoundment, and government by presidential veto. We also examine the attempts by Congress to reassert itself through curbing emergency powers, overseeing executive agreements, monitoring the intelligence agencies, independent budget planning, confirmation politics, and use of the legislative veto. Finally, we look at the Supreme Court decision curbing legislative vetoes and the resulting shift in congressional-presidential relations.

CHAPTER OUTLINE

    I.   CONGRESS VS. THE PRESIDENT: THE BUILT-IN CONFLICT
         A.   Constitutional powers
         B.   Sources of conflict
         C.   Presidential influence on Congress

    II. THE IMPERIAL PRESIDENCY
         A.   Modern expansion of presidential power
         B.   Secrecy and abuse of power during wartime
         C.   Emergency powers and executive agreements
         D.   Presidential veto

    III. CONGRESS REASSERTS ITSELF
         A.   Curbing presidential powers

        1. Warmaking
        2. Emergency
        3. Use of intelligence agencies
        4. Budget reform: Gramm-Rudman-Hollings
        5. Appointments

  IV. SUPREME COURT RESTRICTIONS ON THE LEGISLATIVE VETO
        A. Scope of limitations
        B. Probable results

   V. THE RESURGENT PRESIDENCY?
        A. Restrengthening the presidency?
        B. A more aggressive Congress?
        C. Conflicting trends

PRETEST

1. In comparing constitutional powers granted to the president and to
    Congress, the following generalization is true.

    a. Both are described in   c. Presidential power is
       vague terms.   detailed; congressional power
    b. Congressional powers are   is vague.
       detailed; presidential   d. Both are described in detail.
       powers are vague.

2. In one of the following instances, the War Powers Act does not
    authorize the president to commit the armed forces.

    a. a congressional declaration c. a national majority vote
       of war   d. certain national emergencies
    b. specific statutory
       authorization

3. Critics assert that the presidency became imperial because of the
    ambiguity of the president's _____ power.

    a. domestic   c. military
    b. political   d. leadership

4. President Nixon took revolutionary steps to expand presidential
    powers in all but one of the following ways.

    a. established an extra legal   c. misused intelligence agencies
       investigative force   d. authorized illegal breaking
    b. created a separate   and entering
       military force

                                137

5. The Johnson-Nixon experience as war presidents seems to demonstrate that the public and Congress at the outset of a war are apt to be

   a. apathetic.
   b. bitterly opposed.
   c. highly supportive.
   d. very skeptical.

6. The president enters into secret foreign arrangements without congressional approval by means of

   a. inherent powers.
   b. CIA protocol.
   c. executive agreements.
   d. UN security resolutions.

7. Action of an executive in refusing to spend appropriated funds is called

   a. emergency loan.
   b. executive finance.
   c. pecuniary containment.
   d. impoundment.

8. The War Powers Act appears to have been observed only in

   a. Honduras.
   b. Libya.
   c. Lebanon.
   d. Grenada.

9. The act that was designed to encourage Congress to evaluate the nation's fiscal situation and program-spending priorities in a comprehensive way is

   a. the National Fiscal Act.
   b. the Congressional Appropriations Act.
   c. the Congressional Budget Act.
   d. the Financial and Administrative Control Act.

10. A legislative veto is used by Congress to

   a. block a law signed by the president.
   b. delegate power and then review the results.
   c. to prevent the House from overriding the Senate.
   d. to force congressional unanimity.

PROGRAMMED REVIEW

Knowledge Objective: To examine the role of Congress and the president within a system of checks and balances

1. The Constitution (does, does not) _____ confer policy-making powers on both Congress and the president.

2. Framers of the Constitution expected the president to be dominant in _____ policy.

3. Congress and the president usually (do, do not) _____ work together.

4. Congress and the president are answerable to (the same, different) _____ constituencies.

5. Most members of Congress (are, are not) _____ dependent on presidential support for reelection.

6. In his relationship with Congress, the president normally occupies a (weak, strong) _____ position.

Knowledge Objective: To analyze the argument over the imperial presidency

7. Imperial presidency theorists contend that, although earlier presidents exercised enormous powers in wartime, Johnson and Nixon abused power in _____.

8. Two major events that provoked widespread negative reaction to the imperial presidency were _____ and _____.

9. President Lincoln waged war for several months in 1861 without the consent of _____.

10. Historically, American presidents have sent troops into battle (without, with) _____ the consent of Congress.

11. President Lyndon Johnson succeeded in getting congressional support for his Vietnam policy on the basis of _____ information.

12. President Nixon waged a secret war in _____ during 1969-70 with no formal congressional knowledge.

13. Abuses of presidential power under emergency laws have included the detention of American citizens of _____ ancestry during World War II.

14. The president has been granted vast powers by Congress to control transportation and communication when he declares that an _____ exists.

15. _____ arrangements permit a president to enter into secret arrangements with a foreign nation without Senate approval.

16. The president (does, does not) _____ have item veto power.

17. (Most, Few) _____ presidential vetoes have been overridden.

139

18. Congress can often pass controversial items by attaching _____ to needed legislation.

Knowledge Objective: To examine attempts of Congress to reassert itself

19. The War Powers Resolution of 1973 reflects the determination by Congress to control the president's formerly unlimited discretion to use _____ abroad.

20. The National Emergency Act of 1976 (ends, extends) _____ the extensive powers possessed by the presidency as a result of earlier legislation.

21. Congress recently declared that a state of _____ would automatically end after six months.

22. Congress has attempted to control CIA activities by requiring reports to congressional _____ .

23. Congress has stipulated that the CIA is not to engage in any police work or to perform operations (within, outside) _____ the United States.

24. Secret projects of the CIA are referred to as _____ operations.

25. In an unprecedented exercise of power, Congress amended the defense bill of 1976 to (authorize, end) _____ covert intervention in Angola.

26. Using the concept of _____ , President Nixon refused to spend $18 billion appropriated by Congress.

27. The Budget and Control Act was designed to encourage _____ to make its own budget.

28. The establishment of a Congressional Budget Office has resulted in (reduced, undiminished) _____ presidential budget powers.

29. The 1991 goal of the Gramm-Rudman-Hollings bill is a national deficit of _____ .

30. Recently the Senate has taken a (tougher, more permissive) _____ stand on confirming presidential nominations.

31. The practice whereby a president secures the approval of senators before making an appointment in their states is known as senatorial _____ .

32. The _____ veto is used by Congress to block presidential action.

33. The legislative veto power of Congress was (enhanced, weakened) _____ by a recent Supreme Court decision.

Knowledge Objective: To review the search for a proper balance between congressional and presidential power

34. The American people quite clearly (do, do not) _____ want strong purposeful leadership in the 1980s.

35. Most people believe that Congress (can, cannot) _____ furnish the necessary leadership.

36. President Reagan demonstrated (great, limited) _____ skill in dealing with Congress.

POSTTEST

1. Historically, the main role of Congress has been to

   a. check presidential power.
   b. respond to presidential leadership.
   c. delegate power among its own committees.
   d. all of these.

2. Critics who question the twentieth century evolution of the presidency have named the modern office the _____ presidency.

   a. imperial
   b. dictatorial
   c. fragile
   d. flub dub

3. For much of the twentieth century, scholars held that

   a. we needed a stronger Congress.
   b. we needed to enlarge the number of Supreme Court justices.
   c. we needed a powerful presidency.
   d. all of these.

4. Once a state of emergency has been declared, a president may

   a. seize property.
   b. assign military forces abroad.
   c. institute martial law.
   d. all of these.

5. Although the president may not impound congressional appropriations, much the same result may be achieved by

   a. not issuing bonds.
   b. ignoring legislative vetoes.
   c. deferring payments.
   d. using the item veto.

141

6. The president who impounded billions of dollars of funds appropriated by Congress was

   a. Johnson.   c. FDR.
   b. Nixon.   d. Ford.

7. The president's veto power over bills does not include one of the following actions.

   a. returning it unsigned with   c. taking no action if Congress
      objections   adjourns in 10 days
   b. taking no action for five   d. threatening to veto a bill
      work days   before passage

8. The purpose of the Gramm-Rudman-Hollings bill is to

   a. increase taxation.   c. reduce federal deficits.
   b. increase the national debt. d. cancel the national debt.

9. From 1947 to the mid-1970s, no area of national policy-making was more removed from congressional oversight than

   a. Department of State.   c. CIA.
   b. OMB.   d. NSC.

10. The current status of the legislative veto is that it is

    a. unconstitutional.   c. a powerful weapon.
    b. unimportant.   d. used by the opposition.

POLITICAL SCIENCE TODAY

Leadership   Most Americans are critical of Congress and supportive of presidential leadership. This thesis can be tested at the grassroots by polling a cross-section of Americans (20 people) at a nearby shopping mall, using the following question that has been employed in Gallup polls:

   "Do you think what the country needs is really strong leadership
   that would try to solve problems directly without worrying about
   how Congress or the Supreme Court feels, or do you think that such
   leadership might be dangerous?"

Compare results with other class members. Did most pollsters obtain the same response? What do results show about American attitudes toward the central issue of this chapter?

KEY CONCEPTS

Explain: "Checks and balances; old models and new tests."

Discuss: The impact of Watergate and Vietnam on both
                Congress and the presidency

Explain: How the president acquired so many emergency powers

Analyze: The imperial presidency argument of Schlesinger and
                the counterargument of Lowi

Discuss: Diplomacy by executive agreement

Analyze: The argument for executive privilege

Explain: The Budget and Impoundment Control Act of 1974

Analyze: Why the Gramm-Rudman-Hollings bill is sometimes
                described as a "bad idea whose time has come"

Discuss: The case for a more assertive Congress

Discuss: Implications of the Supreme Court decision holding
                the legislative veto unconstitutional

Contrast: The Carter "terminal meekness" presidency and the
                "muscular" Reagan model

ANSWERS

Pretest

  1. b
  2. c
  3. c
  4. b
  5. c
  6. c
  7. d
  8. c
  9. c
 10. b

Programmed Review

  1. does
  2. foreign
  3. do

4.   different
5.   are not
6.   weak
7.   peacetime
8.   Vietnam; Watergate
9.   Congress
10.   without
11.   misleading
12.   Cambodia
13.   Japanese
14.   emergency
15.   Executive
16.   does not
17.   few
18.   riders
19.   troops
20.   ends
21.   emergency
22.   committees
23.   within
24.   covert
25.   end
26.   impoundment
27.   Congress
28.   undiminished
29.   zero
30.   tougher
31.   courtesy
32.   legislative
33.   weakened
34.   do
35.   cannot
36.   great

Posttest

1.   b
2.   a
3.   c
4.   d
5.   c
6.   b
7.   b
8.   c
9.   c
10.   a

16 Judges: The Balancing Branch

American judges play an active role in our political life, although they are less frequently in the headlines than the president or Congress. In this chapter we focus on the national judicial system. Major attention is directed toward the organization, history, and procedures of the Supreme Court.

CHAPTER OUTLINE

I. THE LAW
    A. Types of law: statutory, common, civil, equity, constitutional, admiralty, administrative, criminal
    B. Scope of judicial power
    C. How judges make law: interpretation and application
    D. The rule of precedent (stare decisis)

II. THE SHAPE OF FEDERAL JUSTICE
    A. District courts: original jurisdiction
    B. Courts of appeal (12): review of decisions
    C. Supreme Court: original and appellate jurisdiction
    D. Special courts
    E. Federal prosecutors (Department of Justice employees representing the U.S. government)
    F. Reforming the federal judicial system (the Burger proposals)

III. WHO ARE THE JUDGES?
   A. Selection process participants: Senate, American Bar Association, political parties, president, Department of Justice
   B. The importance of ideology, race, sex
   C. Judicial philosophy: restraint vs. activism
   D. The Senate Judiciary Committee
   E. A profile of Supreme Court history

IV. HOW THE SUPREME COURT OPERATES
   A. What cases reach the court
   B. Briefs and oral argument
   C. The conference
   D. Writing opinions
   E. Opinions as judicial strategy
   F. Powers of the Chief Justice
   G. Enforcing the Court's decision

V. JUDICIAL POWER IN A DEMOCRACY
   A. The debate over judicial activism
   B. The people and the courts
   C. The complexity of policy-making process

PRETEST

1. Procedure in the Supreme Court is surrounded by considerable ceremony. All but one of the following procedures is customary.

   a. The justices are always attired in their robes of office.
   b. Government attorneys wear morning clothes.
   c. All judges are seated in alphabetical order.
   d. Judges are introduced by the Clerk of the Court.

2. The chief basis for judicial decisions is probably

   a. precedent.
   b. public opinion.
   c. the party in power.
   d. checks and balances.

3. The judicial doctrine of stare decisis provides that the courts decide cases largely on the basis of

   a. present economic and social conditions.
   b. earlier court decisions.
   c. interpreting the will of Congress.
   d. equity.

4. Federal courts of appeal normally have

   a. original jurisdiction.   c. three-judge panels.
   b. grand juries.   d. judges with ten-year terms.

5. No decision can be rendered by the Supreme Court unless

   a. all nine judges   c. six judges participate.
      participate.   d. at least two judges represent
   b. a quorum of five is present.   majority opinion.

6. At the Friday conference of Supreme Court justices, all but one of
   the following is true.

   a. The chief justice presides. c. Each justice carries a red
   b. The chief justice votes   leather book.
      first.   d. A majority decides the case.

7. The powers of the chief justice include all but one of the
   following.

   a. presiding over the Court   c. barring dissenting justices
   b. choosing the opinion writer   from the Friday conference
      if he himself has voted   d. leading conference discussion
      with the majority

8. The "rule of four" in Supreme Court procedure provides that four
   judges

   a. may adjourn the Court.   c. give priority to the order of
   b. grant a writ of Certiorari.   hearing a case.
                                   d. are a quorum.

9. Critics of judicial activism believe that the courts should not try
   to make policy because

   a. judges are not elected.   c. their terms do not coincide
   b. they do not represent all   with that of the president.
      regions of the country.   d. they do not have the necessary
                                      expertise.

10. Attempts to reform the federal judiciary have emphasized one of the
    following.

    a. recruiting better-qualified c. improving administrative court
       judges   procedures
    b. disciplining inefficient   d. ending the appellate juris-
       judges   diction of district courts

PROGRAMMED REVIEW

Knowledge Objective: To describe the differing forms of law on which
the American legal system is based

1. Law based on judicial decisions of medieval English judges is
    _____ law.

2. Law based on judicial interpretation of the Constitution is _____
    law.

3. A specific act of a legislative body is _____ law.

4. Law based on exceptions from the common law in the interests of
    justice is _____ law.

5. The code of law emerging from bureaucratic decisions is _____
    _____ law.

6. The rule of precedent under which federal courts operate is called
    _____ _____.

7. The concept that the courts should serve as a neutral referee
    between two contending parties is called the _____ system.

Knowledge Objective: To gain an overview of the organization of the
federal court system

8. The lowest federal courts, in which nearly 700 judges preside, are
    _____ courts.

9. The federal courts that review district court decisions are courts
    of _____.

10. The highest federal court, with both original and appellate
    jurisdiction, is the _____ _____.

11. The right to review cases already considered is _____ _____.

12. The top U.S. prosecutor is the _____ _____.

13. The chief spokesman for reform of the federal judicial system has
    been former Chief Justice _____.

14. Much of the lower level judicial work of the U.S. district is now
    carried out by _____.

15. A great deal of the demand for reform of the U.S. judicial system
    is prompted by the increasing _____ _____ of the courts.

16. A new court of appeals has been proposed to reduce Supreme Court case load by _____ appeals.

17. The court officer who determines most appeals heard by the Supreme Court is the _____ _____.

Knowledge Objective: To study the major participants involved in selection of federal judges

18. The custom that requires the president to consult with a state's senators before nominating a federal judge is called _____ _____.

19. All potential nominees for federal judgeships are _____ by the American Bar Association.

20. In naming federal judges, the political affiliation of the nominee may be less important than the person's _____.

21. Presidential nominations to the Supreme Court are reviewed by the Senate _____ _____.

Knowledge Objective: To discover how the Supreme Court operates

22. The only cases heard by the Supreme Court are those selected by the _____ _____.

23. Cases previously decided by lower courts are called up to the Supreme Court by writs of _____.

24. The normal upper time limit granted to counsel for each side in arguing a Supreme Court case is _____ _____.

25. Supreme Court decisions are made in secret each week at the _____ _____.

26. One use of published Supreme Court _____ is to communicate with the general public.

Knowledge Objective: To evaluate the role of judicial review in a democratic society

27. Over the past forty years more than 400 acts of _____ and _____ _____ have been invalidated by the Supreme Court.

28. When the Supreme Court becomes greatly involved in political life, it is known as an _____ court.

29. Critics who believe that the Supreme Court has become too activist charge it with engaging in _____ _____.

30. Mr. Dooley declared that the Supreme Court reflected public opinion because it followed the _____ returns.

31. The opponents of judicial activism believe that the Court should not become involved in _____ making.

POSTTEST

1. An activist court, the critics say, is overly zealous in protecting the

   a. poor.
   b. property owners.

   c. state officials.
   d. military officers.

2. The federal court that has only original jurisdiction is

   a. the Supreme Court.
   b. district courts.

   c. courts of appeal.
   d. lower courts.

3. An adversary system of justice is one in which

   a. the police bring charges.
   b. the court is a neutral referee.

   c. judges are political appointees.
   d. justice is based on majority vote.

4. The top national official who has openly favored minority considerations in the judicial selection process has been

   a. Carter.
   b. Burger.

   c. Ford.
   d. Reagan.

5. The law that evolved from decisions interpreting our basic national governing document is

   a. constitutional law.
   b. administrative law.

   c. equity law.
   d. statutory law.

6. Several justices have timed their retirement to

   a. ensure a replacement by a president sharing their views.
   b. increase their retirement benefits.

   c. bring fresh ideas to the Court.
   d. avoid ruling on an issue where they have no competence.

7. Elections eventually influence Supreme Court decisions because

a. the judges try to do what the people want.
b. judges who are out of step are impeached.
c. new judges are appointed.
d. interest groups influence decisions.

8. In federal courts, justiciable disputes are

a. all constitutional questions.
b. those involving actual cases.
c. all administrative decisions.
d. those involving political questions.

9. The relationship between the state and federal court systems is

a. federal courts are always superior.
b. state courts have original jurisdiction.
c. they have interrelated responsibility.
d. they are completely separate.

10. If a Supreme Court justice agrees with the majority decision but differs on the reasoning, he files

a. a concurring opinion.
b. a dissenting opinion.
c. articles of agreement.
d. a minority opinion.

POLITICAL SCIENCE TODAY

1. Judicial Profile   Choose one of the major figures in our judicial history and secure the following facts about him:
   a. What was his family and educational background?
   b. What was his work experience before his court appointment?
   c. Why was he selected?
   d. What attitudes characterized his decisions on the court?

2. Profile of a Current Judge   Investigate one of the current members of the Court, using the same criteria. Begin with Who's Who in America and then look for additional information.

3. Making Abortion Policy   Review the facts and decision in Roe vs. Wade (1973), and the subsequent decision of 1983 that expanded the right of women to have abortions. Discover what efforts are currently being made at the local, state, and national levels to reverse that decision. This should result in a paper showing the relationship between individuals, the Supreme Court, the president, the Congress and state legislatures, interest groups and nurses, doctors, and hospitals.

KEY CONCEPTS

Identify: Six different categories of the law applied by the
                    federal courts

Explain: The adversary system

Describe: How judges make laws

Define: Stare decisis and describe how it determines
                    judicial decisions

Differentiate: Between district courts and courts of appeal

Describe: The job of a federal prosecutor

Explain: How former Chief Justice Warren Burger proposes to
                    reform the federal court system

Discuss: a. The selection of federal judges as a bargaining
                        process
                    b. The Reagan belief in selecting judges on a
                        partisan basis
                    c. The role of ideology in the selection of judges

Construct: A step-by-step account of how a typical case might
                    move through the federal court system, including
                    the processing of the case by the Supreme Court

Explain: Judicial activism and criticisms leveled against
                    this judicial philosophy: The Court's role in
                    policy making

ANSWERS

Pretest

  1. c
  2. a
  3. b
  4. c
  5. c
  6. b
  7. c
  8. b
  9. a
 10. c

Programmed Review

1. common
2. constitutional
3. statutory
4. equity
5. administrative
6. stare decisis
7. adversary
8. district
9. appeal
10. Supreme Court
11. Appellate jurisdiction
12. Attorney General
13. Burger
14. magistrates
15. work load
16. screening
17. solicitor general
18. senatorial courtesy
19. evaluated
20. ideology
21. Judiciary Committee
22. Supreme Court
23. certiorari
24. thirty minutes
25. Friday conference
26. opinions
27. legislatures; city councils
28. activist
29. judicial legislation
30. election
31. policy

Posttest

1. a
2. b
3. b
4. a
5. a
6. a
7. c
8. b
9. c
10. a

17 Bureaucrats: The Real Power?

Most activities of the federal government are carried out by bureaucrats. Hence the selection, organization, and control of these people is a central issue of government. Today most elected officials join the public in being critical of the bureaucrats and bureaucracy. President Reagan promised to curb the bureaucracy by eliminating the Departments of Education and Energy, cutting pay raises and fringe benefits of workers, and placing a ceiling on the number of federal employees. His Grace Commission, in its final report, claimed that $424 billion could be saved in three years by carrying out its 2,478 recommendations. Critics scoffed! Supporters cheered!

CHAPTER OUTLINE

    I. THE SHAPE OF THE FEDERAL BUREAUCRACY
        A. The bureaucrats (3 million civilians, widely dispersed)
        B. Formal organization arranged by function
        C. Informal organization based on personal relationships

   II. THE U.S. CIVIL SERVICE
        A. Merit system
        B. Hatch Act and political activity

  III. BUREAUCRACY IN ACTION
        A. Classical model: rationality
        B. "Real" model: political implications

C. Illustrative case studies: J. Edgar Hoover, Admiral
    Rickover, George Brown

IV. CRITICISMS OF BUREAUCRACY
     A. Widespread cultural hostility
     B. Major criticisms: mushrooming growth, red tape, waste and
         inefficiency
     C. Grace Commission and bureaucratic waste
     D. The basic questions: responsiveness and accountability

V.   CONTROLLING THE BUREAUCRATS
     A. Shared control: president, Congress, courts
     B. Civil Service Reform Act (1978) created a senior executive
     C. Patronage system support
     D. OMB: management control
     E. Congressional attempts at control

PRETEST

1. Depending on the observer, red tape can be described in all but one
    of the following ways.

    a. senseless regulations that   c. an established procedure for a
        prevent prompt action   particular operation
    b. civil service employees   d. a bureaucracy that is more
        who serve under the merit   interested in means than ends
        system

2. Almost half of all civilian employees of the federal government
    work for

    a. defense agencies.   c. welfare agencies.
    b. the Social Security   d. the Interstate Commerce
        Administration.   Commission.

3. Most independent agencies of government are created by

    a. the president.   c. the Cabinet.
    b. Congress.   d. the Domestic Council.

4. An example of a government corporation is

    a. the Securities and   c. the Government Printing
        Exchange Commission.   Office.
    b. the U.S. Mint.   d. the Domestic Council.

5. The independent regulatory boards have all but one of these special characteristics.

    a. They do not report directly   c. Their members are political
       to the president.   appointees whose terms
    b. They perform legislative   coincide with the president's.
       functions.   d. They have judicial functions.

6. A landmark law creating a merit system of civil service was the congressional act named for its sponsor.

    a. Garfield   c. Pendleton
    b. Sedman   d. Hatch

7. The OPM plays all but one of the following roles in recruiting new civil service employees.

    a. administers and scores   c. creates a ranked register of
       tests   successful applicants
    b. designates the individual   d. certifies three names for each
       an agency must hire   agency vacancy

8. President Nixon attempted to change the administrative structure so that

    a. each agency had greater   c. it would reflect broad
       freedom.   national goals.
    b. agency recruiters could   d. taxes were cut by elimination
       hire outside the Civil   of agencies.
       Service Commission.

9. The classical model of public administration theory emphasized all but one of the following.

    a. friendship patterns   c. chain of command
    b. line and staff   d. span of control

10. The weakest relationship of most federal administrators is with

    a. fellow colleagues.   c. congressional committees.
    b. lobbyists.   d. the president.

PROGRAMMED REVIEW

Knowledge Objective: To examine the shape of federal bureaucracy

1. Bureaucrats are accused of being inefficient and too _____ at the same time.

2. Nearly _____ of all federal civilian employees work for the defense agencies.

3. Over 85 percent of the bureaucrats work _____ the Washington area.

4. Most federal employees are _____ collar workers.

5. The federal level of bureaucracy has (grown, decreased) _____ in the past few years.

6. Federal employees are _____ representative of the nation as a whole than legislators.

7. The common basis for organization of a department is _____.

8. An example of a government _____ is the Tennessee Valley Authority.

9. _____ organization emphasizes structure; _____ organization emphasizes personal relationships.

Knowledge Objective: To trace the evolution of the U.S. Civil Service

10. The _____ system permitted newly elected presidents to appoint their supporters.

11. Restrictions on the political activities of federal employees were imposed by the _____ Act.

12. Federal employees (may, may not) _____ take an active part in partisan politics.

13. _____ _____ was a noted German sociologist who advocated an efficient, nonpolitical bureaucracy.

14. Under the "real bureaucracy" model, civil servants are involved in the _____ of policy.

Knowledge Objective: To analyze the criticisms of bureaucracy

15. Most Americans support bureaucracy that operates in their interest while being critical of big bureaucracy in the _____.

16. There are _____ federal civil servants per 1,000 Americans today than there were a generation ago.

17. The major recommendation of the Grace Commission that President Reagan implemented was _____.

18. The _____ of a federal agency is the _____ rather than the rule.

157

19. One major problem of big government has been that _____ exceed performance.

20. The complex rules and regulations under which bureaucracy functions is called _____ _____ .

Knowledge Objective: To discover the controls under which bureaucrats operate

21. Major control of bureaucracy is shared by _____ and the _____ .

22. The Civil Service Reform Act (1978) created a top grade of career bureaucrats, the _____ _____ _____ .

23. _____ laws authorize an agency to function for a set number of years.

24. Supporters of the patronage system believe that the existing _____ system of federal employment encourages deadwood.

25. _____ is the executive office responsible for managing the federal bureaucracy.

26. The responsiveness of bureaucrats is limited by the procedures that make them _____ .

POSTTEST

1. The largest subunit of a government department is usually called a

   a. bureau.   c. commission.
   b. division.   d. cabinet.

2. Using the choices (a) more or (b) less than, compare the federal bureaucracy today with that of thirty years ago on (1) expenditures as percentage of GNP; (2) number of civil servants per 1,000 Americans.

3. Congress normally controls the bureaucracy in all of the following ways except

   a. budgetary appropriations.   c. confirmation of personnel.
   b. holding hearings.   d. firing civil servants.

4. Only one of the following terms does not describe the same model of public administration.

   a. textbook   c. classical
   b. incremental   d. rational man

5. An example of informal organization would be when a superior and his subordinates

   a. hunt and fish together.
   b. confer over bureau policy.
   c. jointly evaluate employees for promotion.
   d. establish long-range budget plans.

6. Who controls the bureaucracy?

   a. the president
   b. Congress
   c. no single power source
   d. the voters

7. Sunset laws are best defined as requirements that

   a. all government meetings be public.
   b. bureaucrats must retire at sixty-five.
   c. all requests for information must be answered in 48 hours.
   d. all agencies must justify their existence every seven years.

8. The Grace Commission did not recommend one of the following actions to reduce government waste.

   a. fewer, but better administrators
   b. strong presidential veto powers
   c. improved accounting procedures
   d. increased user fees

9. The responsiveness of a bureaucracy is closely linked to its

   a. accountability.
   b. security.
   c. clientele.
   d. computer capability.

10. The most accurate evaluation of the impact of federal employee unions is that they

   a. often call unjustified strikes.
   b. regularly negotiate higher salaries.
   c. refuse to answer to congressional committees.
   d. represent workers in grievance proceedings.

POLITICAL SCIENCE TODAY

1. <u>Civil Service</u> One employer that many college students are interested in is the federal government. Secure answers to the following questions regarding the federal service?
   a. When and where are civil service examinations given in your region?

b. What is the average starting salary for college graduates?
c. How is promotion determined?
d. Assuming average advancement, what salary and fringe benefits would a person be eligible for in ten years?
e. How do these standards compare with those of private industry?
f. Would you recommend that any of your friends consider a federal position? Why or why not?
g. What change do you feel would be most apt to make the federal service more attractive?

2. <u>Bureaucratic Structure</u> Your own college or university is a close-at-hand example of bureaucratic structure. Produce an organizational chart that shows the relationship between the president and the superior governing body on the one hand and the internal structure on the other. Are there other bodies that have authority? A faculty union? A senate? A student government? Other unions? How do they fit on the chart? Where is policy made? Where is final authority lodged?

KEY CONCEPTS

<u>Construct</u>:   The personal profile of a typical bureaucrat

<u>Differentiate</u>:   Between formal and informal organization, with an example of each

<u>Evaluate</u>:   The common charges against bureaucrats

<u>Prove</u>:   That the federal bureaucracy is mushrooming or that it is a "no growth" area

<u>Discuss</u>:   The idea that we should abolish red tape and let bureaucrats make decisions based on good judgment

<u>Trace</u>:   Efforts to depoliticize the civil service

<u>Differentiate</u>:   Between the classical and real bureaucracy models

<u>Describe</u>:   How the careers of three federal bureaucrats illustrate realities of the bureaucratic world: J. Edgar Hoover, Hyman Rickover, George Brown

<u>Contrast</u>:   The ways in which Presidents Nixon, Carter, and Reagan proposed to make the bureaucracy more responsible

<u>Discuss</u>:   "Americans seem to invoke Jeffersonian values-- decentralization, local control, small and amateur

government--more insistently as these values become more obviously irrecoverable."

Discuss: "Government is not the solution to our problems; government is the problem."

Discuss: "We need to get the bureaucracy off our backs and out of our pocketbooks."

Analyze: Strengths and weaknesses of the Grace Commission Report

ANSWER

Pretest

1. b
2. a
3. b
4. d
5. c
6. c
7. b
8. c
9. a
10. d

Programmed Review

1. powerful
2. half
3. outside
4. white
5. decreased
6. more
7. function
8. corporation
9. formal; informal
10. spoils
11. Hatch
12. may not
13. Max Weber
14. politics
15. abstract
16. fewer
17. privitization
18. death; exception
19. promises
20. red tape

21. Congress; President
22. Senior Executive Service
23. sunset
24. tenure
25. OMB
26. accountable

Posttest

1. a
2. a, b
3. d
4. b
5. a
6. c
7. d
8. a
9. a
10. d

18 The Democratic Faith and the Necessity of Politics

The bed-rock foundation of any government is the set of assumptions upon which it is founded. Democracy has its own special beliefs about the ability of people in general, the role of leaders, and the goals of government. Too often, in our day-to-day study of government's nuts-and-bolts, we skip over the basic ideas underlying the whole system. American students find it especially hard to stand off and look critically at their own government's philosophical underpinnings. Yet this ability is at the very core of political wisdom. It is useful to remember that most people who have lived on the planet Earth have been subject to authoritarian rulers. Our government is one of the rare exceptions, constantly faced with the question as to whether "this nation or any other nation so conceived and so dedicated can long endure".

Although American democracy is often described as "government by the people", we actually depend heavily on leaders to give focus and direction to the nation. Therefore, competent leadership becomes a key factor in making the political system work. The sources of this leadership, the way in which leaders make their way to the top, and the qualities that make for great leadership are basic questions which students of government must consider. In our history, who are the leaders that loom large? Do some periods call forth great leaders, or do great leaders make their own times?

CHAPTER OUTLINE

I. PHILOSOPHICAL ASSUMPTIONS AND PARADOXES
   A. Faith and skepticism about majority rule
   B. Majority rule, minority rights, checks and balances
   C. Historical norm of authoritarian rule

II. THE AMERICAN DREAM
   A. Lack of well-defined ideology
   B. Contradictory beliefs
   C. Long-standing, worldwide aspirations: peace, prosperity, personal property, liberty
   D. Components of the American Dream
      1. Opportunity
      2. Rugged individualism
      3. Practical experimentation
      4. Faith in the people's common sense
      5. Government as a necessary evil
      6. Messianism, ethnocentrism, sense of mission
      7. The American Way and the American Dream
      8. Criticisms: materialism, legalism, irresponsibility

III. RESTORING THE AMERICAN DREAM: WHICH DIRECTION?
   A. A central question: Do we have too much freedom or too little equality?
   B. Curbs on the majority and on government's power: Bill of Rights
   C. Built-in inefficiency
   D. Expanded definition of liberty with aid from government: jobs, housing, education, medical care
   E. Excessive demands on government
   F. Balancing competing demands and rights

IV. PARTICIPATION AND REPRESENTATION
   A. Limits of direct democracy: federalism, separation of powers
   B. Types of representation: political parties, Congress, president
   C. Broker rule versus majority rule

V. AMERICAN ATTITUDES TOWARD POLITICAL LEADERS
   A. The traditional love-hate relationship
   B. Public's low ranking of politicians in honesty and ethics
   C. How politicians emerge

VI. WHAT KIND OF LEADERSHIP?
   A. Types of leaders
      1. Movement catalyzers (agitators)
      2. Coalition builders
      3. Office holders
      4. Managers vs. leaders

B. Politicians as brokers
  1. Wheeler-dealer image
  2. The democratic principle of compromise
  3. The roles of ambition and opposition
  4. Independent, questioning citizens
  5. Transformational vs. transactional leadership

VII. THE DEMOCRATIC PROMISE
  A. Freedom of expression and dissent
  B. Need for good newspapers and sound schoolmasters
  C. Need for continuous, active citizenship
  D. Experimental approach
  E. Search for effective leadership
  F. Unity and diversity

PRETEST

1. The American people rank as least ethical one of the following groups.

   a. funeral directors   c. TV reporters
   b. stockbrokers   d. politicians

2. American politicians tend to win their great acclaim

   a. shortly after election.   c. after death.
   b. while running for office.   d. when they win reelection.

3. If the political scene is thought of as a three-act play, one set of players would not be regarded as

   a. fund raisers.   c. coalition builders.
   b. crowd gatherers.   d. balancers and bargainers.

4. At the very heart of those personal characteristics that motivate politicians is

   a. ideology.   c. selfishness.
   b. ambition.   d. craftiness.

5. The American Dream is most easily attainable by

   a. women over 50.   c. hard-working Hispanics.
   b. white Anglo-Saxon males.   d. high I.Q. Blacks.

6. Americans have traditionally believed that economic success was the result of

   a. our abundant natural resources.
   b. self-help.
   c. government programs.
   d. luck.

7. Identify the unrelated word.

   a. rugged individualism
   b. materialism
   c. resourcefulness
   d. humanitarianism

8. Direct democracy works best when

   a. an area is small.
   b. a society is pluralistic.
   c. people are well-educated.
   d. standards of living are high.

9. Participatory democracy works best in

   a. colleges.
   b. cities.
   c. states.
   d. the armed forces.

10. Broker rule is best described as

   a. compromises between conflicting groups.
   b. substituting interest groups for parties.
   c. regulation by the New York Stock Exchange.
   d. giving women greater power.

PROGRAMMED REVIEW

Knowledge Objective: To analyze the American Dream of democracy

1. According to democratic theory, the only legitimate foundation for any government is the _____ of the people.

2. The democratic concept in practice is a mixture of _____ and _____.

3. In the full span of human history, most people have lived under _____ rule.

4. The great American champion and spokesman for democracy in the late eighteenth century was _____ _____.

5. Jefferson believed that governments were bound to degenerate that trusted _____ alone.

6. John Adams believed that democracies were inevitably destroyed by _____.

7. In America government has always been regarded as a necessary _____.

8. The belief that Americans are a chosen people with a special destiny is called _____.

9. Americans believe that their country is (superior, similar) _____ to other nations.

Knowledge Objective: To review the basic guiding principles of American democratic government

10. _____ was the principle most valued by the framers.

11. The Constitution both _____ and _____ power to national, state, and local governments.

12. The Constitution distributes power between the _____ and _____ governments.

13. Efficiency (was, was not) _____ the main goal of the framers.

14. The framers tried to protect individual liberty _____ government.

15. The major competing values that dominate American government today are _____ and _____.

Knowledge Objective: To examine the prospects for American democratic government

16. Individual needs and the needs of society must be _____.

17. Negotiations between interest groups within the Congress that result in compromise legislation is called _____ rule.

18. Democratic governments always have _____ groups that are free to speak out.

19. Rather than dogma and theories, American democracy has emphasized _____ and _____.

20. In contrast to citizens of democracies, who are expected to think for themselves, citizens of authoritarian states are expected to _____.

21. American citizens (are, are not) _____ normally critical of their government.

Knowledge Objective: To analyze American attitudes toward politicians

22. Americans yearn for leadership, but they also want to be _____ _____.

23. Politicians are held _____ in public esteem.

24. The public tends to be (most, least) _____ critical of politicians that they know personally.

25. We probably expect too (much, little) _____ of politicians.

Knowledge Objective: To define the various kinds of leadership

26. An example of a movement catalyzer is _____ _____ who was a conservative advocate of tax cutting.

27. Coalition builders differ from movement catalyzers in that they are chiefly interested in _____ _____.

28. As political brokers, the coalition builders try to work out _____ between divergent groups.

29. The heart of democratic politics is _____.

30. Competing groups force most politicians to become _____.

Knowledge Objective: To identify the various kinds of leadership

31. Managers and leaders (do, do not) _____ require the same skills.

32. _____ leaders are those whose vision attracts others to strive for new goals.

33. Effective leaders rely on _____ rather than power.

34. There (is, is not) _____ a single effective style that all leaders should learn and practice.

35. The leaders who emphasize bargaining and compromise are called _____.

Knowledge Objective: To consider politicians as actors and brokers

36. Act I political leaders who "stir things up" are called _____ _____.

37. Act II political leaders who galvanize movements are called _____ builders.

38. Act III political leaders normally are _____ _____.

39. Elected officials in the political drama normally play a role as _____.

40. _____ lies at the very heart of politics.

POSTTEST

1. The principal objective of the framers was

   a. efficient government.   c. individual liberty.
   b. representative government.   d. responsive representatives.

2. The virtues of our present political system include

   a. easy leadership.   c. decisive action.
   b. safeguards against tyranny.   d. quick response to majorities.

3. The framers were least interested in making the government

   a. moderate.   c. safe.
   b. balanced.   d. efficient.

4. Alexander Solzhenitsyn declares that modern America has all but one of the following defects.

   a. materialism   c. moral commitment
   b. timid leadership   d. permissiveness

5. Only one of the following national figures was skeptical about the potential and ability of the common man.

   a. Harry Truman   c. Walt Whitman
   b. Abraham Lincoln   d. John Adams

6. The full operation of majority rule is slowed by all of the following except

   a. federalism.   c. Bill of Rights.
   b. free elections.   d. checks and balances.

7. Identify the unrelated word.

   a. righteousness   c. sense of mission
   b. messianism   d. isolation

8. In writing the Constitution, all of the following goals were sought
   except

   a. efficiency.
   b. competing constituencies.
   c. distribution of power.
   d. preservation of strong local governments.

9. Leaders who emphasize power depend on

   a. force.
   b. persuasion.
   c. eloquence.
   d. charisma.

10. To have a democratic society, one of the following practices must exist.

   a. the right to dissent
   b. total press freedom
   c. no restrictions on obscenity
   d. government-funded abortions

POLITICAL SCIENCE TODAY

1. Aspiring Leaders: Draft a profile of one of the following national spokesmen who is outside the serious contenders for the presidency:
   Andrew Young
   Jerry Falwell
   Lyndon LaRouche
   Pat Robertson
   Federico Pena
   Henry Cisneros

   What basic group supports this leader? What evidence exists to show support beyond this base group? Why and how is this person's visibility projected? What financial base does he have? Has he attempted coalition building? Under what handicaps does he operate?

2. Local Leaders: Use your home congressional district as a base to do a political analysis of leadership in that area, using 1980 census data. What is the reported population by sex? By national origin? By race? How is that population distribution reflected by national office holders? State office holders? County office holders? Major city officials?

3. The American Dream: Prepare an annotated bibliography of ten popular books published during the past decade that are concerned with the current American political, social, and economic scenes.

   As a second step, write a short essay that summarizes the tone of this bibliographical list. Is it optimistic? Pessimistic? Contradictory? How does current writing about the American future

170

compare with the long-standing hopes and aspirations that make up the American Dream?

KEY CONCEPTS

Discuss: The built-in conflict between rugged individualism
                    and the expanded definition of liberty to include
                    jobs and medical care

Describe: The messianic characteristics of American ideology
                    and its impact on our foreign relations

Suggest: How unity and diversity can both be accepted as
                    American goals

Debate: America today is a soft, decadent, floundering
                    nation that has lost any central sense of direction

Describe: Why the text authors believe that no freedom should
                    be absolute

Suggest: A quick test to discover if a government is
                    democratic

Describe: The strategies used by the framers to preserve
                    liberty from government action

Indicate: The tensions that exist in modern society between
                    our two goals of liberty and equality

Explain: Why we like politicians whom we know, make national
                    heroes out of those who are dead, yet disparage
                    political leaders as a group

Discuss: Why we condemn politicians for bargaining and
                    compromising

Analyze: Why American politicians resort to broker rule
                    rather than standing on principle

Differentiate: a. Between transactional and transformational
                        leadership
                    b. Between power and authority

171

ANSWERS

Pretest

1. d
2. c
3. a
4. b
5. b
6. b
7. d
8. a
9. a
10. a

Programmed Review

1. will
2. faith; skepticism
3. authoritarian
4. Thomas Jefferson
5. rulers
6. themselves
7. evil
8. messianism
9. superior
10. liberty
11. grants; withholds
12. national; state
13. was not
14. against
15. liberty; equality
16. balanced
17. broker
18. minority or opposition
19. pragmatism; experimentation
20. obey
21. are
22. left alone
23. low
24. least
25. much
26. Howard Jarvis
27. winning elections
28. compromises
29. compromise
30. brokers
31. do not
32. Transformational
33. authority

34. is not
35. brokers
36. agitators
37. coalition
38. elected officials
39. brokers
40. compromise

Posttest

1. c
2. b
3. d
4. c
5. d
6. b
7. d
8. a
9. a
10. a